The Mysterious Case of the
Mary Celeste

150 YEARS *of* MYTH AND MYSTIQUE

GRAHAM FAIELLA

The mystery of the *Mary Celeste*. (*Shipping Wonders of the World*, 19 January 1937)

First published 2022

The History Press
97 St George's Place, Cheltenham,
Gloucestershire, GL50 3QB
www.thehistorypress.co.uk

British Library Cataloguing in Publication Data.
A catalogue record for this book is available from the British Library.

ISBN 978 0 7509 9815 4

Typesetting and origination by The History Press
Printed and bound in Great Britain by TJ Books Limited, Padstow, Cornwall.

Trees for Lyfe

Contents

Preface

In truth, there was nothing unusual about the discovery of an abandoned sailing ship, adrift in the North Atlantic, in the nineteenth century. Hundreds of derelicts were recorded every year. Some drifted around for months, even years. Eventually, though, they simply broke up from the abuse of their watery wandering, or ended up wrecked.

But some were not left derelict. Some, when found, were taken by the finders for the prize of a potentially lucrative payday as salvage.

In December 1872 the discovery of one of these oceanic waifs was most unusual. The derelict was still under sail, which was odd enough. She seemed to be shipshape; somewhat shabby and sailing erratically, but otherwise in pretty good order. There was no one on board, which, still, was not odd: she was a derelict!

What *was* strange was that, as the finders who boarded her soon realised, there seemed to be no earthly reason why the crew had abandoned her.

A handful of men from the vessel that found the derelict halfway between the Azores and the coast of Portugal put her rigging in order, pumped the water out of her and sailed her to Gibraltar. Their own ship had arrived at Gibraltar the day before and put in a claim for salvage of the derelict when she arrived. The inquiry into the claim, to determine the salvage reward, was heard by a Vice-Admiralty Court over three months. It included the testimony of eyewitnesses who had found the derelict about the condition of the vessel when they boarded her, and others with interests in her. Eventually a salvage award was made to the finders.

The derelict had since been made seaworthy and shipshape, and had taken on a new crew. She carried her cargo to her original destination of Genoa, on the Ligurian coast of Italy. She sailed on for another dozen or so years, under different owners. Early in 1885 she was wrecked, suspiciously, on a reef off Haiti.

That ship was the *Mary Celeste*.

The reason why the ten people on board deserted her, and what happened to them, has become one of the great unsolved mysteries of the sea. From that enigmatic act of desperation 150 years ago there has sprouted a prolific (some might say profligate) garden (some might say veritable prairie) of myth and mystique.

A ghost ship, some have said. But the real ghost of the *Mary Celeste* is the truth about *why* she was abandoned. Relatively watertight, seaworthy solutions to that mystery have been floated by creative and fanciful and sometimes logical speculation over the decades, but have never anchored in a fair haven of certainty.

In truth, it has been a search for *the* truth. And that – the pursuit, and, as often, dereliction and perversion of truth – is the real story of the *Mary Celeste*.

Acknowledgements

I'm most grateful to Commissioning Editor Amy Rigg at The History Press for inviting me to write this book. From it, to my surprise, have emerged insights into the nature, manipulation and infectious corrosion of truth, as much as my investigation reveals the story, mythology and mystique of the great mystery of the *Mary Celeste* from 150 years ago.

PART I

THE MYSTERY

'Anything can happen at sea.
And usually does.'

Anon.

Origins of the Mary Celeste

The *Mary Celeste* wasn't always the *Mary Celeste*. More or less the same ship, yes, but she had a different identity from when she was born, so to speak, by the time she set sail on her mystery voyage of 1872.

So: to begin at the birthing.

Up at the northern end of the Bay of Fundy, the waterway that splits the island province of Nova Scotia to the east from mainland Canada to the west, there was, in the mid-nineteenth century, a small settlement called Spencer's Island. The Glasgow-born Scots-Canadian journalist, historian, photographer and author Frederick William Wallace (1886–1958) described the place in his biography of square-rigged merchant ships in what was then British Canada, *In the Wake of the Wind-Ships* (1927):

> Spencer's Island and its Ships
> At the head of the Bay of Fundy, and where Cape Spencer and Cape Split stand on opposite shores as portals to the Basin of Minas, one will find the small settlement of Spencer's Island a short distance to the northward of the cape of the same name. The place is named after a little island which lies about a quarter of a mile off the mainland of Cumberland County, Nova Scotia.
>
> Spencer's Island is so small a place that it will only be found upon a topographical map of the county, but in shipping annals it is remarkable for the smart shipmasters it sent forth and for the particularly fine class of sailing ships built there. In numbers there were

> not many, but practically all the Spencer's Island craft were noted for their fast passages. All were registered at Parrsboro, N.S. [about 25 miles/40km away to the east] …
>
> The first vessel to be built at Spencer's Island was the brigantine *Amazon*, 198 tons, which was launched in May 1861 by Joshua Dewis.

Dewis was born near Spencer's Island. As a shipbuilder 'in his early manhood', he conceived the idea of setting up a shipbuilding business when he moved nearer Spencer's Island sometime in the late 1850s. There, with like-minded neighbours, he built a modest little vessel named the *Amazon*. She was launched in May 1861 and duly registered at nearby Parrsboro. *Amazon* was the first ship to be built at Spencer's Island (and the only one by Joshua Dewis), and she was the first incarnation of the *Mary Celeste*.

Amazon was a handspan over 99ft long, from her stem to her stern; her width, 25ft, and her depth, 11½ft. Her gross registered tonnage was 198.42.

And she was rigged as a brigantine.

The brigantine *Amazon* at Marseilles, November 1861, by unknown artist.

Nauticalia

It's necessary here to say a word or two about ships' measurements and other nautical esoterica relating to ships' rigging. In a number of respects, a basic familiarity about this will be helpful in understanding certain particulars that crop up in the myth and mystery of our *Mary Celeste*.

TONNAGE

The term 'tonnage', as most *generally* applied to a ship, is not a measure of *weight*. It is a *volume* measure of the internal space of a vessel, in cubic feet, divided by 100. *One ton register* is 100 *cubic feet* (f^3). So a ship of 198.42 registered tons, as *Amazon* was, is not equivalent to the weight of forty elephants but more like the volume of forty buses.

Gross register tonnage is the total volume of enclosed space within a ship, including her cargo holds, cabins and rooms to accommodate crew and passengers, the engine room (if any), deck-house and so on, as determined by an official survey. Deducting all the space in a ship that costs, rather than earns money (the latter being the hold or holds in which she carries her freight of cargo; the former being everything else), what is left is the space of her cargo-carrying capacity: her *net registered tonnage*.

The comparison of ships by size is usually in terms of *gross registered tons* (or GRT), as well as by their length from stem to stern (which excludes the length of a bowsprit, the pole pointing out from the stem of a sailing ship or boat, with sails attached to it), their width (or *beam*) at their widest point, and their depth (which is most simplistically from the bottom of the ship's hull to her main deck).

RIGGING AND SHIP TYPES

One of the niggling little tics that has infested the shaggy dog stories about the *Mary Celeste* has been whether she was a *brig*, or a *half-brig*, or a *small brig*, or a *hermaphrodite brig* – or a *brigantine*. *Amazon* right from the start was rigged and officially registered as a brigantine. As *Mary*

Celeste, she was also a brigantine. But even to some people who were otherwise knowledgeable about maritime matters, and to many others who wouldn't have known a fid from a fiddle, she was a kind of brig – small, half or hermaphrodite – or a brigantine, depending on where they got the name from.

BRIGANTINE.

Brigantine.—The true brigantine is a two-masted vessel having a fully square-rigged fore-mast, and a fore-and-aft rigged main-mast with square-sails on the topmast. This rig does not seem to have been used to any great extent, and the term brigantine is now used to describe such a vessel as above, but without the main topsails.

See below.

HERMAPHRODITE BRIG.

Hermaphrodite Brig.—This rig has a fully rigged fore-mast, and fore-and-aft rigged main; it is the same as the true brigantine but without the square topsails on the main. The term hermaphrodite brig is no longer in use and this rig is now known as a brigantine.

Brigantine rigs. (Harold Underhill, *Sailing Ship Rigs and Rigging*, Brown, Son & Ferguson, 1938)

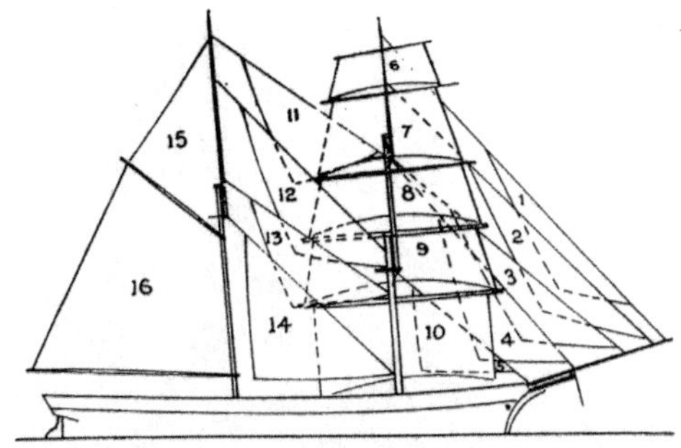

SAILS OF A BRIGANTINE. (Hermaphrodite-brig.)

1. Flying-jib.
2. Fore-topgallant-staysail or outer-jib.
3. Jib.
4. Fore-topmast-staysail.
5. Fore-staysail.
6. Fore-royal.
7. Fore-topgallant.
8. Fore-upper-topsail.
9. Fore-lower-topsail.
10. Fore-sail or fore-course.
11. Main-topgallant-staysail.
12. Main-topmast-staysail.
13. Middle-staysail.
14. Main-staysail.
15. Gaff-topsail.
16. Main-sail, spanker or driver.

Brigantine sails. (Harold Underhill, *Sailing Ship Rigs and Rigging*, Brown, Son & Ferguson, 1938)

A brig, in effect, was colloquial shorthand for any small, 200–300-ton or so vessel with two masts, one or both of which was square-rigged. The truth about brigs and brigantines in those days isn't that they were as different as cats and dogs, but that they were more like cocker and springer spaniels. Technically, though, and correctly, *Amazon/Mary Celeste* was a brigantine.

In a simplified characterisation:

A *brig* is a sailing vessel with two masts – the *foremast* towards the bow, the *mainmast* behind it – both of which are rigged with square sails (*square-rigged*).

A *brigantine* also has two masts but is square-rigged only on the foremast and fore-and-aft rigged on the mainmast. It was sometimes, away in the past, called a *hermaphrodite brig* because it was both square- and fore-and-aft rigged, and similarly a *schooner brig*, because it was *fore-and-aft rigged* on its mainmast, like a schooner.

FIG. 96. A HERMAPHRODITE BRIG, COMMONLY BUT ERRONEOUSLY CALLED A BRIGANTINE.

Hermaphrodite brig, or brigantine. (E. Keble Chatterton, *Sailing Ships and Their Story*, Sidgwick & Jackson, 1909)

'A. Ansted', the author of the estimably comprehensive *A Dictionary of Sea Terms* (1920), defined 'fore-and-aft' as: '*in the direction of a line drawn from stem to stern of a vessel*; that is, from the forward or *fore* to the after or *aft* part'; and explained that: 'Such sails as yachts and sailing boats carry are fore-and-aft sails; and such as are set in a direction *across* the ship are called *square sails*, constituting the *square rig* of most merchant [sailing vessels].'

(Ansted also included in his dictionary a term he defined with particular wit and, one suspects, first-hand experience: 'Sea sickness.– A malady which, though originating at sea, receives but scant sympathy thereon.')

The *gaff mainsail* on a brigantine is the big four-sided fore-and-aft mainsail on the mainmast. Along its upper edge the sail is attached to the *gaff*, a pole extending from the mast-side corner of the sail to its uppermost outer end, the *peak*. Sailors on deck hoist the gaff, and sail, by ropes, the *halyards*. The halyards that raise the outermost peak end of the gaff, usually attached at two points along it, are the *peak halyards*, an important detail in one of the proposed 'solutions' to the mystery of how, if not why, the *Mary Celeste* might have been abandoned.

Amazon had a single topsail on her foremast, the topsail being the second square sail up from the big square sail (or *course*) at the lowest level of a ship's mast. Single topsails were very big, and a devil to handle in a rip-snorter of a storm on a bucking-bronco sea with their steel-hard canvas stretched taut by the wind. They were nail-rippingly treacherous for sailors to furl up on the yardarm on a dark and stormy night (or any time, come to that).

By the latter decades of the nineteenth century, the single topsail was most commonly divided into two smaller and therefore more manageable lower and upper topsails, to ease the plight of sailors for whom, never mind 'one hand for the ship, one for yourself!', it was 'both hands for the ship and hold on the best you can with your legs!' in order to control the bigger single topsail of earlier times.

Amazon was a single-topsail ship. That rig was later changed to smaller double topsails when she became the *Mary Celeste*, a minor but salient detail of the condition of her when she was found abandoned.

The brigantine-rigged *Amazon* was owned in shares of 64ths, as was the Nova Scotian custom of the day. Her builder, Dewis, was the biggest shareholder with a 16/64ths stake. Eight others – local farmers, mariners and merchants – each had between 4 and 8/64ths interests.

Amazon was a trim and well-built ship, not particularly speedy in the manner of the big clipper ships but of good, sturdy Nova Scotian shipbuilding pedigree. She was a utility vessel, a work-horse hauling her freights of cargo around the Canadian Maritime provinces, along the Eastern Seaboard of the United States, through the West Indies and Gulf of Mexico, and back and forth across the Atlantic.

A painting of her at Marseilles by an unknown artist in November 1861 was done when she came into the French Mediterranean port at that time, the same year she was launched. The picture clearly shows the big single topsail on her foremast later divided into two smaller topsails on the *Mary Celeste*.

On 9 November 1867, on a voyage out of Halifax, *Amazon* was driven ashore in a gale at a place called Cow Bay (now Port Morien) on Cape Breton Island, a notoriously hazardous region for ships at the northern end of Nova Scotia. There followed a series of ownership changes, starting with a Cape Breton 'gentleman', Alexander McBean, who was by then the sole owner of all the shares in the salvaged ship.

Eventually *Amazon* was sold to a succession of New Yorkers. By the end of 1868 her sole owner then, Richard Haines, an American, had been granted a change of nationality for the ship from British to American under a new identity as the *Mary Celeste*. There seemed to have been, allegedly, a bit of jiggery-pokery about how the *Mary Celeste* obtained her American registry. Nevertheless, and by whatever means, by 1869 she had evolved from the Nova Scotian-born British-flagged brigantine *Amazon* of Parrsboro to her newly acquired nationality, flying the Stars and Stripes as the American brigantine *Mary Celeste* of New York.

A year later, in January 1870, after another series of ownership changes, shares in the *Mary Celeste* were divided between four men. Capt. James H. Winchester, a New York shipmaster who had a few years earlier retired from the sea to set up as a ship broker, agent and owner, owned a 4/8ths stake in her. Capt. Winchester and his shipping company, J.H. Winchester & Co., of New York, would play a prominent role in and after the *Mary Celeste*'s mystery voyage of 1872.

By the end of October 1872, a few weeks before the start of that voyage, Capt. Winchester still owned the one-half share of the *Mary Celeste*. Amongst the other three part-owners was Capt. Benjamin Spooner Briggs, with a one-third holding of 8/24ths that Capt. Winchester had sold to him on the condition that Briggs take command of the *Mary Celeste*.

Capt. Winchester had by then known Capt. Briggs for some time, as master of some of his ships. J.H. Winchester & Co. was agent for Benjamin's brother Oliver's own ship, the brig *Julia A. Hallock.* He knew the quality of the man he now enjoined to take his brigantine and her cargo from New York to Genoa as an experienced, honest and peer-respected sea captain of twenty years' standing. His *Mary Celeste,* he surely reckoned, would be in a safe pair of well-seasoned hands.

Capt. Benjamin Spooner Briggs

Capt. Benjamin Spooner Briggs, master of the *Mary Celeste,* 1872.

Yankee shipmasters from New England weren't always a model of decorum and rectitude in the way they ran their ships and crews. Capt. Benjamin Spooner Briggs, by all accounts, was. He came from a family brined in the seafaring tradition: four of his father Capt. Nathan Briggs' five sons, including Benjamin, went to sea, 'and two ... became master mariners at an early stage'.

Capt. Nathan Briggs was spartan in his ship management: a disciplinarian, but fair. His teetotal principle of 'No grog will be allowed on board' from his earliest years as a sea captain was written into the articles of contract for all the crews he signed on his ships. His son, Capt. Benjamin Briggs, continued the practice on ships he later commanded.

Nathan was born in 1799 and had gone to sea early, as was the custom in those times. He commanded his first ship, the schooner *Betsy & Jane,* at the age of 21. He married his first wife, Maria Cobb, in 1827. She died just over a year later in 1828.

Two years later Capt. Nathan married Maria's sister, his sister-in-law, Sophia Matilda Cobb (born 28 October 1803 at Rochester, near Wareham on the Massachusetts coast). They had six offspring: Maria, the first, in 1831; then Nathan, Benjamin, Oliver, James and the youngest, Zenas. James was the only son not to go to sea as a profession, becoming a businessman in nearby New Bedford. Even first-born Maria was wedded to the sea, by marriage.

Benjamin Spooner Briggs was born at Wareham, Massachusetts, on Buzzards Bay across from and just south of Cape Cod, on 24 April 1835. His mother, Sophia Cobb, was the daughter of a Congregational church minister, the Rev. Oliver Cobb. After her husband Capt. Nathan suffered 'severe financial reverses' towards the end of the 1830s, from a failed investment in Wareham, Sophia and three of her children, including young Benjamin, then about 4 years old, were obliged to move into Rev. Cobb's parsonage home at Marion, nearby along the coast.

By 1844 Capt. Nathan had redeemed his finances sufficiently to allow himself and his family to move into a new home, 'Rose Cottage', at Sippican Village, a mile or so away from the parsonage at Marion.

Young Benjamin's upbringing there was within a Christian and disciplined family, 'redolent of the sea', and strongly influenced by mother Sophia, 'a woman of strong character whose Christian faith enabled her to withstand, with grace and fortitude, the successive shocks caused by the loss at sea of two sons and a daughter by shipwreck; two sons by yellow fever while at sea and by the death of her husband, Captain Nathan, struck by lightning as he stood in the doorway of their home'.[1]

The two sons who died at sea of yellow fever were: Benjamin's older brother Nathan H. Briggs, mate on a ship that sailed out of Galveston, Texas, in 1855, when he died three days out and was buried at sea; and the youngest Briggs boy, Zenas, who was mate on his older brother Oliver's ship, the brig *Julia A. Hallock*, and died as the *Hallock* was coming into port in North Carolina, in October 1870. This was not long after patriarch Capt. Nathan himself was struck and killed by lightning, on 28 June 1870, standing in his 'Rose Cottage' doorway.

The only daughter of Sophia and Capt. Nathan was Maria. In 1856, aged 25, she married a family friend, Joseph Gibbs, yet another seafarer amongst the extended Briggs clan. Maria often sailed with husband Capt. Joseph. Both were drowned after their ship collided with a steamer off North Carolina in November 1859.

On 9 September 1862, Benjamin married his cousin, Sarah Elizabeth Cobb. Sarah was the daughter of her mother Sophia's brother, the Rev. Leander Cobb who performed the marriage ceremony in his Congregational church at Marion. Sarah was 20 years old; Benjamin was 27. Their first-born, in 1865, was named Arthur, ostensibly after the ship Capt. Benjamin then commanded. Their only other child, Sophia Matilda, named after her grandmother, was born on 31 October 1870. When Capt. Briggs took command of the *Mary Celeste* two years later, he and Sarah agreed that Arthur, then aged 7, would stay at home at 'Rose Cottage' to get on with his schooling. Two-year-old Sophia would accompany them on the Genoa voyage.

Capt. Benjamin Briggs was already a seasoned sea captain by the time he married Sarah in 1862. They honeymooned in Europe on board the schooner he then commanded, the *Forest King*. She later accompanied her husband on ships he commanded, as she would when he captained the *Mary Celeste* for the first and only time in 1872.

The 1872 Mystery Voyage

In the months just before that fateful voyage, as she lay at New York, the *Mary Celeste* was modified in certain respects. The main changes were that she now had two decks, having previously had just the one. Her length was increased from 99ft to 103ft, her width, slightly greater than her original 25ft, and her depth from 11.7ft to just over 16ft. Her tonnage increased from just under 200 to just over 282, by the enlargement of her cargo hold and cabins for the crew and Capt. Briggs and his wife and daughter.

Her bottom was sheathed in copper, a common remedy in those days to protect a wooden ship's hull from the dreaded teredo worm that bore into the wood like termites and compromised a ship's seaworthiness.

And what had been *Amazon*'s single topsail was changed to two, a lower and upper topsail, on her *Mary Celeste* foremast.

After Capt. Briggs left home at Marion, he arrived in New York on 19 October 1872 to oversee the preparations and loading of the vessel he would soon be commanding on her transatlantic voyage to Genoa. By 2 November, the *Mary Celeste* had loaded a cargo of 1,701 casks of alcohol. This was a type of denatured industrial-grade alcohol, used for the fortification of certain wines. It was certainly not drinkable on its own as sailors' grog, even if the crew had been hard-bitten or foolish enough to try. And the *Mary Celeste*'s crew were neither. The cargo only filled about half the expanded hold space of the vessel.

The alcohol cargo was owned by a German trading firm in New York, Meissner, Ackerman & Co., for delivery to the Genoa firm of

H. Mascarenhas & Co. 'The value of the cargo, said to have been insured abroad, was reported as £6,522-3-0 [$37,000].'[12]

The voyage was undertaken by the *Mary Celeste*'s agent and majority owner, J.H. Winchester & Co. The insurance on the ship's hull, split amongst four companies, totalled $14,000. The freight, or charter value of the voyage – the amount J.H. Winchester would earn from the transport of the consignment of alcohol to Genoa – was $3,400. That value was insured against the risk of non-delivery with the Atlantic Mutual Insurance Company. These are all details that would be central to the salvage claim hearings at Gibraltar, to determine the monetary reward for salvaging the abandoned *Mary Celeste*.

The Crew

Apart from 37-year-old Capt. Briggs, the crew of the *Mary Celeste* on her Genoa voyage comprised seven men: a first and second mate, a cook-cum-steward, and four ordinary seamen.

First mate Albert G. Richardson, aged 28, was from Stockton Springs, Maine. He was related by marriage to Capt. Winchester as the husband of his wife's niece. Winchester characterised him as 'a man of excellent character'. He had also previously sailed under Capt. Briggs and in Capt. Winchester's ships for about two years before he signed on the *Mary Celeste*. Capt. Briggs noted to his wife that, with mate Richardson, they would be in 'good hands'. He was, in short, a seaman held in high regard. His wife, Frances (Fannie), lived to a sprightly 91 years before her death in Brooklyn, New York, on 29 April 1937.

Second mate was a 25-year-old New Yorker, Andrew Gilling, about whom not much else is known. It is possible, from later correspondence by his mother in Denmark, 'regarding news of his fate', that he had a Danish background.

The steward-cum-cook was Edward William Head, a native New Yorker from Brooklyn, aged 23 and only recently married to his wife, Emma. The rest of the crew, the ordinary seamen, were Prussian-German:

Volkert Lorenzen, 29; his brother Boz, 25; Arian Martens, 35; and Gottlieb Goodschaad (or Goodschaal), 23.

Sarah Briggs wrote a letter to her mother-in-law, Sophia, from on board the *Mary Celeste*, dated 7 November. It was shortly after the start of the voyage (and the last communication ever from the ship) as they were anchored off Staten Island, waiting for favourable weather to proceed. She noted that her husband 'thinks we have got a pretty peaceable set [crew] this time all around if they continue as they have begun. Can't tell yet how smart they are.' However smart they might have been, they certainly weren't the ruffians, possibly homicidal, that they were later characterised as by some myth-spinners.

The *Mary Celeste* was indeed crewed by a good 'set'. As author Charles Edey Fay has remarked: 'it seems reasonable to assume that Captain Briggs, experienced mariner that he was, would exercise more than ordinary care in the selection of a crew for a voyage on which his wife and two-year-old daughter were to accompany him'.

With his cargo loaded and stowed by the evening of Saturday, 2 November, Capt. Briggs signed his crew on at the offices of the United States Shipping Commissioner on Monday, 4 November, intending to depart the next day. The names of all the crew were thereby certified on the usual Articles of Agreement that contracted them and outlined the conditions of their employment. Over the following decades their number and names were variously fictionalised, corrupted and calumniated. But the evidence of how many and who they were was clearly documented: seven crew, plus Capt. Benjamin Spooner Briggs, his wife Sarah and 2-year-old daughter Sophia, all present and accounted for.

Apart from overseeing the final preparations of his ship, Capt. Briggs had been keeping a lookout for the expected arrival at New York of his brother Oliver in his own ship, the *Julia A. Hallock*, before the *Mary Celeste* sailed. Oli, as he was known, had left Malaga, southern Spain, towards the end of September. Six weeks later, in mid-November, the *Hallock* arrived in New York, about a week too late for Oli's and Benjamin's anticipated reunion.

She sailed again at the end of the month for Gijón in north-west Spain, and arrived there on Christmas Eve. The intention was for the Briggs brothers to be reunited at Messina in southern Italy when the *Hallock* and the *Mary Celeste* were scheduled to be there around the same time in or around February of 1873. It was a tentative plan for the only two remaining seafaring sons of mother Sophia; more tenuous, indeed, than either could have imagined.

Departure of the Mary Celeste

Some of the items brought on board the *Mary Celeste*, apart from provisions and stores, included: the crew's sea chests of clothing and personal effects; the captain and his wife's clothing and accoutrements; toys for 2-year-old Sophia; Sarah Briggs' melodeon – a kind of small piano – with books of sheet music; and her sewing machine and related items (thimble, thread, needles, 'a small phial of oil').

There was also on board an old, partly rusted sword and its scabbard sheath, presumed to have been owned by Capt. Briggs. This would later become an important and controversial article of close scrutiny in the subsequent investigation at Gibraltar, not to mention in the mythification of the *Mary Celeste* mystery later on.

What was never mentioned as having been brought on board, and so presumably was not, was a cat, which only emerged later in some of the mythical Scotch mists of the *Mary Celeste*.

Mary Celeste was cleared for sailing by the New York port authorities on Tuesday, 5 November 1872. Capt. Briggs was anxious to get going, to keep to the schedule of delivering his consignment of alcohol to Genoa and onward loading of another cargo for the *Mary Celeste* to take on at Messina. Strong north-easterly headwinds, however, obliged him to anchor off Staten Island for a few days until the weather improved.

On Thursday, 7 November, the *Mary Celeste* weighed anchor under fair skies and light winds. Pilot Burnett, a New York harbour pilot, got her into safe water, took letters from the ship to be mailed ashore, collected his pilotage fee and no doubt bid Capt. Briggs a safe voyage. He was the last person ever to see the ten souls aboard the *Mary Celeste* as she slipped away into the Atlantic and became 'The Greatest Sea Mystery'.

The *Dei Gratia*

About a week after the *Mary Celeste*'s departure, another brigantine, the *Dei Gratia*, sailed on 15 November from New York for Gibraltar 'for orders', meaning that her master, Capt. David Morehouse, would get instructions there about where to deliver her consignment of 1,735 barrels and 499 cases of petroleum (oil and other liquid cargoes were carried in those days in round barrels and square cases).

Dei Gratia was slightly bigger than the *Mary Celeste*: 295 tons compared with the *Mary Celeste*'s 282; 111ft long, 28ft wide and 13ft deep. She was a new ship, built in 1971 near the settlement of Bear River on the south-west Bay of Fundy coast of Nova Scotia, and registered as

The brigantine *Dei Gratia* in 1873.

from Bear River. Like the Nova Scotian *Amazon* built further up the bay a decade earlier, she was British-flagged.

Capt. David Reed Morehouse, aged 34, had been a sea captain, like Benjamin Briggs, from his early 20s. He was Nova Scotia-born, at a place called Sandy Cove, just down the coast from Bear River, on 22 March 1838. His first mate on the *Dei Gratia* was a near neighbour from south-west Nova Scotia, Oliver Deveau, born on 9 September 1837, a year older than Capt. Morehouse. Deveau, too, was an experienced seaman and had already been in command of a vessel.

The rest of the known crew of the *Dei Gratia* were second mate John Wright and ordinary seamen Augustus Anderson, John Johnson and Charles Lund. Two other *Dei Gratia* seamen were of unknown identities (who, in any case, contributed no subsequent public evidence or information about the *Mary Celeste* incident). That made a total ship's complement of eight, the same number of crew, including Capt. Briggs, as the *Mary Celeste*'s.

Dei Gratia logged heavy weather on her voyage across the Atlantic, which was reported to have been 'in an unusually tempestuous mood' of 'very heavy seas and winds of gale force' at that time. In fact, the North Atlantic was quite typically stormy towards the late autumn months, some years more so, some less. Neither the *Mary Celeste*'s nor the *Dei Gratia*'s masters, Briggs and Morehouse, would have been unduly disconcerted; heavy weather was an accepted trial of any seafarer's competence.

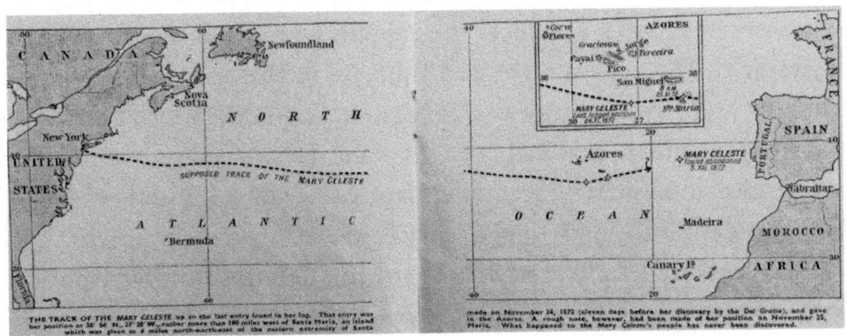

The transatlantic track of the *Mary Celeste*. (*Shipping Wonders of the World*, 19 January 1937)

At least by the *Dei Gratia*'s reckoning, her voyage was 'devoid of unusual incident'. Until, that is, Monday, 4 December. She had by then passed north of the Portuguese archipelago of the Azores and was approximately half way between the Azores and the coast of Portugal, steering east-south-east towards Gibraltar, around 600 miles away. That day, however, a decidedly 'unusual incident' guaranteed the *Dei Gratia*'s inclusion – indeed, momentous importance – in the *Mary Celeste* annals.

Early on the afternoon of 4 December, second mate John Wright was the officer of the watch. Two seamen were on deck with him, Augustus Anderson and, steering at the *Dei Gratia*'s wheel, John Johnson. Capt. Morehouse was also on deck. A sail was sighted 4 or 5 miles away to the east of the *Dei Gratia*, just about on the horizon. Capt. Morehouse took a look at her through the 'glass', or telescope.

She was, he saw, heading westward, in the opposite direction to the *Dei Gratia*, under 'short canvas', meaning with only a few sails set. She was sailing quite slowly, at just 1 or 2 knots, and erratically, as he wrote in the *Dei Gratia*'s log: 'steering very wild and evidently in distress'. And, like his own vessel, she was a brigantine. More ominously, there seemed to be no one on deck.

Capt. Morehouse called first mate Deveau up on deck to take a look and see what he thought. They both agreed that the stranger seemed to be in some kind of distress, although she flew no distress signals. Capt. Morehouse altered course for the *Dei Gratia* to approach her. When the two brigantines were near enough, he hailed her but got no response. At around 3 o'clock, the captain sent a boat over to investigate, with Deveau, Wright and Johnson in the boat. The sea was 'running high' from stormy weather earlier, but moderating. The wind was from the north, as it had been for some days.

Contrary to some later accounts, Capt. Morehouse himself never set foot that day on the deck of the *Mary Celeste*.

Deveau and Wright went on board the derelict to look around. Johnson stayed in the boat alongside. After about half an hour, the three men returned to the *Dei Gratia*. Deveau reported to Capt. Morehouse on their cursory examination of the vessel. He confirmed that there was indeed no one on board, and relayed to the *Dei Gratia*'s master other 'most significant things that met the eye during their brief inspection'.

These included the most important detail of all, that she was the brigantine *Mary Celeste* of New York, 'from New York for Genoa, abandoned with 3½ft. of water in [her] hold', according to Capt. Morehouse's logged note of the incident.

'Sea Time'

One particular about the *Dei Gratia*'s encounter with the *Mary Celeste* was that it happened on 4 December 1872, by *civil* time, but on 5 December 1872 by *sea time*. Mate Deveau himself later testified that Capt. Morehouse called him up on deck after sighting the *Mary Celeste* in the early afternoon of '5th December Sea time'.

The term *sea time* derived from the navigational imperative of establishing a ship's daily position at noon (and for establishing when shipboard noon itself was). To this day, a vessel's *day's run* – the distance she covers in a twenty-four-hour day – is from noon to noon, not midnight to midnight or between any other hours of the day.

The convention in bygone years was for a ship to use 12 o'clock noon as the dividing line between one calendar day and the next, which is to say whenever the sun was either due north or due south of a ship on any given day. That was the reference time for her day's run, or distance covered in twenty-four hours. The reference point could not be midnight because there was no sun to observe at that hour! Any time *before* that *navigational noon* was on a date that changed to the next day's date *after* that *navigational noon*. And that form of date-keeping was *sea time*. It was, however, only a convention for noting in the ship's log. For practical purposes in running the ship, the usual civil times and dates were used.

So: the encounter between the *Dei Gratia* and the *Mary Celeste* happened, for practical purposes, in the early afternoon of 4 December 1872.

Log Positions

Mate Deveau noticed two other things of particular significance when poking around the *Mary Celeste*. The first was that the ship's official log book, which he found in the mate's cabin, had been fully written up till 24 November. The latest position recorded in that log was latitude 36° 56' N, longitude 27° 20' W, which was just south of the main group of islands in the Azores and some 120 miles due west of the island of Santa Maria, the south-easternmost island.

The second was that in the captain's cabin he found the 'log slate'. This was used to record daily bits of information that would later go into the ship's official log book. The last entry on the log slate was made at 8 a.m. on 25 November. It recorded that the ship was then just north of the island of Santa Maria. The eastern point of that island 'bore 6 miles [was 6 miles distant] – SSW [to the south-south-west]'.

It also recorded that the *Mary Celeste* was heading on a course 'E. by S.' (east by south), which was just a bit south of due east. And that the wind was from the west, almost, but not quite, coming from directly behind her; blowing, in fact, just a bit over her starboard or right-hand side, so that she would have been on *starboard tack* (more about that later).

When the *Dei Gratia* met the *Mary Celeste* on 5 December, 'sea time', or 4 December by the usual civil calendar, their position was, by 'dead reckoning' of the *Dei Gratia*'s position (meaning that it was a guess based on the ship's course or heading, and speed and therefore distance since their last known or DR position), at '38° 20 N. Lat [Latitude] 17° 15 West Longitude'.

That 5 (or 4) December position was roughly half way between the Azores and the coast of Portugal, and an estimated 380 miles from the *Mary Celeste*'s last recorded position near Santa Maria ten days before. The abandoned derelict had sailed at least, and possibly more than, 380 miles in that time, on her own, with no one on board to steer or work the sails and navigate – assuming that the ten persons aboard her jumped ship at some time soon after the last log slate entry on 25 November.

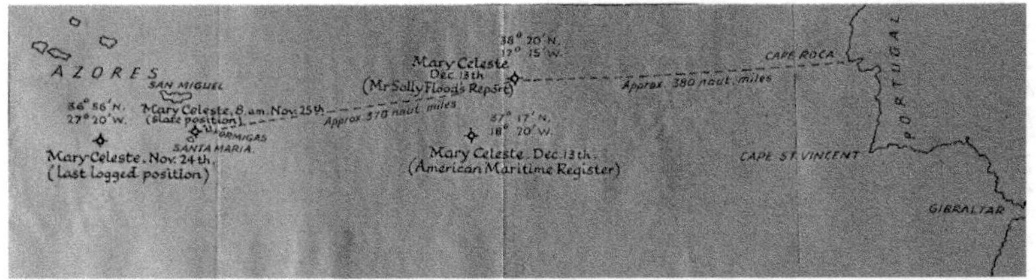

Mary Celeste positions from 24 November to 4 December 1872 (J.G. Lockhart, *A Great Sea Mystery*, Philip Allan & Co., 1930). Lockhart recorded on his chart diagram two positions of the *Mary Celeste* when found by the *Dei Gratia*: the northernmost and correct one, from 'Mr Solly Flood's report' in the subsequent salvage inquiry at Gibraltar; and the second, to the south, as incorrectly stated by the American Maritime Register. He also incorrectly put the date of her discovery by the *Dei Gratia* (4 December) as 'Dec. 13th'. This was actually the date that the *Mary Celeste* arrived at Gibraltar.

At the time the *Dei Gratia*'s men went on board the *Mary Celeste*, they found that the derelict had her big mainsail and various other smaller sails down, most of which were furled and secured. On the foremast the big foresail, the lowest one on the mast, and the upper topsail, the third sail up, were blown away and in tatters. The only way such sails could be shredded like that would be by a strong wind before they could be taken in and secured. The other sails on the foremast, the two topgallants above the two topsails and, highest up, the royal, were all taken in and furled along their yardarms.

The only sails up on the vessel were two of her three jib-like sails set from the foremast to the bowsprit, one of which was her fore-topmast staysail, and also the lower topsail on her foremast, which mate Deveau later described as 'hanging by the four corners'.

So the *Mary Celeste* was far from being 'under full sail' as later 'fake news' narratives had it. The sails she did have set, and those she had down and secured, indicated that Capt. Briggs might have reduced sail because of some boisterous weather, but not including the big foresail and upper topsail found shredded and loose and presumably blown out after the vessel was abandoned. There had indeed been stormy weather around 24 and 25 November when the *Mary Celeste* was just to the south of the main islands of the Azores.

Mary Celeste when encountered by the *Dei Gratia*.

But there might have been another reason for Capt. Briggs to take in sail: to slow his ship down.

Mate Deveau consulted with Capt. Morehouse about what to do with the *Mary Celeste*. It was decided to put three men on her to sail her to Gibraltar, where they would lodge a claim for whatever salvage reward the *Dei Gratia* would get from her. Deveau himself would go as the designated derelict ship's captain. He chose two seamen, Augustus Anderson and Charles Lund, to accompany him on the 600-or-so-mile run to Gibraltar. That left Capt. Morehouse with just four men, including second mate Wright, to manage their own ship in getting to Gibraltar.

The weather at the time was not particularly threatening. The stretch of water from their position to Gibraltar was not known for being particularly treacherous. Under normal circumstances for either the *Dei Gratia* or *Mary Celeste* it would have been a fairly straightforward run of four or five days. But the circumstances to hand were far from normal. It was a risky undertaking for both ships with a skeleton crew that ordinarily required twice as many hands.

The compensation for taking that risk was the possibility of a payout of salvage for the *Mary Celeste* and, of greater value, her cargo of 1,701 casks of alcohol.

The first thing the three *Dei Gratia* men did on the *Mary Celeste* was pump the 3½ft of water out of her bilges and set the rigging and sails in order, which took, all told, two or three days. The two brigantines sailed together in fine weather until the Straits of Gibraltar. Stormy weather thereabouts compelled Deveau on the *Mary Celeste* to separate from his own ship and shelter along the North African shore until the weather moderated. *Dei Gratia* anchored in the Bay of Gibraltar on 12 December 1872. *Mary Celeste* and her three-man crew arrived early the following morning, on Friday, 13 December.

Gibraltar Court of Inquiry

As was the practice with derelicts, the *Mary Celeste* was immediately arrested, to keep her in port pending the outcome of the inquiry into the claim of salvage made by 'David Reed Morehouse, Master of the British brigantine *Dei Gratia* and for the Owners, Officers and crew of the said brigantine, claiming as Salvors'.

Then began proceedings that would involve the scrutiny of eyewitness testimonies, intense forensic investigation, colourful characters and even more colourful – indeed, inflammatory – insinuations that would ignite the first flames of controversy about the mysterious abandonment of the *Mary Celeste*.

The inquiry was held under the auspices of a Vice-Admiralty Court. It was conducted over several months, though with several interruptions, including for surveys of the *Mary Celeste*. It started on 18 December 1872 and ended on 14 March 1873. The aim of the court was to examine the circumstances of how the *Dei Gratia* found and salvaged the *Mary Celeste*, in order to determine the amount of salvage reward, if any, that might be awarded to the salvors.

It would try to determine, too, if possible, why the vessel was abandoned, and what happened to the ten souls who left her – how, indeed, The Greatest Sea Mystery came to be.

The presiding judge of the court was Nova Scotian-born Sir James Cochrane, Attorney General of Gibraltar from 1830 until 1841, and subsequently Chief Justice for Gibraltar until he resigned in 1877.

Queen's Proctor, Mr Frederick Solly-Flood

Gibraltar's Attorney General at the time, Mr Frederick Solly-Flood (or Solly Flood), was titled in the *Mary Celeste* inquiry to suit the rather pompous public servant he was reputed to be: 'Her Majesty's Advocate-General and Proctor for the Queen in Her Office of Admiralty'. (The title 'Proctor' applied to a lawyer acting in Admiralty or ecclesiastical courts in civil law cases, on behalf of the British monarch in their official Admiralty capacity.)

Frederick Solly-Flood, 71 years old at the time, was English-born of Irish ancestry, having inherited his maternal grandfather's estates in Co. Wexford. By at least one account, and intimated probably by others, he was a fuss-pot panjandrum functionary 'whose arrogance and pomposity were inversely proportional to his IQ'.

Born the son of a London fishmonger as Frederick Solly on 7 August 1801, he appended his Irish surname of Flood by 'Royal licence' (so-called 'letters patent') after his father's death in 1820, from his maternal grandfather, the Irish peer, politician and lawyer, Sir Frederick Flood. When Sir Frederick died in 1824, the now Mr Solly-Flood inherited his Irish properties and, presumably, at least part of his fortune. In the same year he married a pastor's daughter, Mary Williamson, who died in 1864. He was educated at Harrow School, graduated from Trinity College, Cambridge in 1825, and was called to the bar in 1828. He set up a legal practice in London, which gambling debts later forced him to sell.

A letter by a great-grandson, in 1969, characterised Solly-Flood as 'born with many golden spoons [who] squandered the lot'. An obituary of his death, in May 1888, remarked that 'his legislative achievements at Gibraltar were numerous and grotesque, including among other things a law upon currency which no one could understand and no one would obey'. He was said to be very fond of 'bathing at Rosea Bay', and when about to plunge into the sea, stood 'in the morning sun absolutely nude except for a pair of *caleçons*'.

By 1866 the colourful Mr Frederick Solly-Flood had 'squandered' his coffers to such an extent, and despite having had an active and respectable, if not particularly lucrative career in England as a barrister, that he accepted the post of Attorney General of Gibraltar. And then, into his jurisdiction, sailed the *Mary Celeste*. And the Solly-Flood imagination about the cause of her abandonment went into overdrive.

Not to be outshone by the luminance of Solly-Flood in the *Mary Celeste* case (though most, in fact, would be) were a host of other players. Mr Henry Pisani was 'Advocate and Proctor for David Reed Morehouse, master of the British brigantine, *Dei Gratia*, and for the owners, officers and crew of the said brigantine, claiming as salvors'. The registrar of the court was Mr Edward Joscelyn Baumgartner. A London lawyer practising in Gibraltar at the time, Mr George Cornwell, acted as Proctor for the owner of the *Mary Celeste*, Capt. Winchester, as claimant for the vessel. Another lawyer, Mr Martin Stokes, was Proctor for the claimants – the owners – of the vessel's cargo of alcohol.

Proceedings began on 18 December 1872. The testimony of the first and by far most the important witness was the *Dei Gratia*'s mate Oliver Deveau:

> 'I am Chief Mate of the British Vessel *Dei Gratia*. I left New York on the 15th November, bound for Gibraltar "for orders." Captain Morehouse, Master. On the 5th December Sea Time, being my watch below, the Captain called me and said there was a strange sail on the windward bow, apparently in distress, requiring assistance. That was probably about 1:00 P.M. Sea Time. I came on deck and saw a vessel through the glass – she appeared about 4 or 5 miles off.'

Deveau thereby set the opening scene of the discovery of the derelict and unmanned *Mary Celeste* on 4 December 1872. The continuation of his testimony mainly concerned what he found when he and second mate John Wright boarded her. Other crew members from the *Dei Gratia* who went on board the *Mary Celeste* also testified to the court at various times.

Amongst others appearing in the drama, although not all in court, were, for diverse reasons: Capt. James Winchester, principal owner of the *Mary Celeste*; Horatio Jones Sprague, the US Consul at Gibraltar from 1848 until his death in 1901 (Sprague was born in Gibraltar in 1823 – he never actually lived in the United States – as his father, from Boston, had set up a 'commission business' there and was himself Consul between 1832 and his death in 1848); and the *Dei Gratia*'s master, Capt. Morehouse. The commander of a visiting American warship, Capt. R.W. Shufeldt, was a minor but important player, though only on behalf of Consul Sprague, not for the pleasure of the court.

But it was Oliver Deveau's statements that gave the most compelling and comprehensive evidence about the state of the derelict when they first boarded her. That evidence, over the following decades, was both a key to understanding the *Mary Celeste* mystery and equally corrupted, contorted, reimagined and mythologised by future narratives. What mate Deveau included in his testimony, given over three different dates, established the truest first-hand eyewitness account of the condition of the *Mary Celeste* when the *Dei Gratia* found her.

What Deveau's observations and those of his crew did *not* include was just as important, considering later assertions by *Mary Celeste* mis-chroniclers of things about the derelict that were pure invention. In the round, though, they were as accurate an audit of the *Mary Celeste*'s condition as any on record.

Combining all the testimonies of the Vice-Admiralty Court about the state of the *Mary Celeste* when she was found, in the interest of brevity, constitutes a kind of *Mary Celeste* mystery salmagundi. The following would be amongst the main components.

On Deck

BILGE WATER

The first thing Deveau did when he and his second mate, John Wright, boarded the *Mary Celeste* was to *sound*, or take a measure of how much water she had in her bilges. This was done through the *pump-well*, a pipe leading from the main deck into the hold, just behind the mainmast, where hand pumps were used to pump out any water in her bilges that accumulated over time.

Soundings of the water in a ship were often taken once every four-hour watch, or at least several times a day, especially in wooden ships more prone to leaking. A metal bolt of about a foot or so in length, the *sounding rod*, was let down on a line through the pump-well to its lowest depth. When it was drawn back up, the depth of any water in the bilges was indicated by wetness on the metal rod and line, similar to a dipstick's indication of the oil level in a car's engine.

Deveau testified that, when he first boarded the *Mary Celeste*, he found the sounding rod on the deck 'lying alongside the pumps'. There was nothing to indicate anything wrong with the pumps, just that the sounding rod had been used and left on deck rather hurriedly.

The very first thing he did, he said, 'was to sound the pumps which were in good order', and he found 'three feet and a half of water in the pumps on sounding them'. That, as it happened, was not much. It certainly didn't indicate a particularly leaky ship. It did, however, suggest to Deveau that, after a crew member of the *Mary Celeste* had sounded the pump-well, they 'found perhaps a quantity of water in the pumps at the moment, and thinking she would go down, abandoned her'.

Charles Lund, who went on the *Mary Celeste* to Gibraltar with mate Deveau and Augustus Anderson, testified that 'The *Dei Gratia* made more water than the *Celeste*.' Anderson also testified to the general seaworthiness of the *Mary Celeste*: 'The vessel was in a fit state to go round the world with a good crew and good sails.'

DISHEVELLED RIGGING

Many of the lines of the running rigging of the derelict – the ropes used to manage and manipulate the sails, spars and yardarms – were in a pretty shambolic condition. Some were hanging over the side of the ship. The main peak halyard, fastened to the outermost end of the mainsail gaff (which was found down and securely furled along its boom), was 'broke and gone', by Charles Lund's testimony. That detail of a 'broke and gone' peak halyard became significant in at least one proposal for how the *Mary Celeste* might have been abandoned.

SAILS

How much sail to set during the voyage of a sailing ship was up to the experience of the captain and officers of a ship, to maintain the good stability, handling and safety of the vessel, but also its speed, according to weather and any other pertinent circumstances. By and large, the stormier and windier the weather, the more sails would be hauled down and secured, to be reset as the weather improved. But how much canvas to keep flying also depended on the temperament of the captain and such particular circumstances as might influence his decisions – such as having a wife and young daughter on board, with a commensurate degree of prudence for the concern of their safety as much as for the safety of the ship herself.

When the *Dei Gratia* met her, the *Mary Celeste* was sailing under *short canvas*, meaning with only a few sails up. These were two of her foresails rigged from the foremast to her bowsprit, and her lower topsail on the foremast. The upper topsail and big foresail seemed to have been set beforehand as well, but were blown out and in tatters when the *Dei Gratia* found the derelict. All the other sails on the vessel were down and mostly well secured.

SHIP'S BOAT

Mary Celeste had apparently carried just one boat. There were davits (a pair of light cranes between which a ship's boat is hung and from which to launch and hoist it back in) at her stern, but they only had a spar, or pole of some kind, lashed across them to keep them steady. The boat seemed to have been kept lashed on top of the deck-house around the middle of the ship.

There was no sign of it or of any other boat when the *Dei Gratia* men went on board her.

The boat might have been launched in a hurry by removing a small section of the rails (sometimes referred to as 'topgallant rails') that surrounded the deck of the *Mary Celeste*, which she had instead of gunwales (solid planking of the ship's side raised above and encompassing the main deck) and which were supported at intervals by stanchions (wooden posts). This would have made a gap through the rails big enough to get the boat over the side. That possible launch gateway, as it were, was what mate Deveau testified to in his last appearance before the court on 4 March 1873:

> 'When I went on board I found the rails on both sides lying on the deck lashed or fastened at one end ... The rails fits in tight in the socket and it takes some force to remove or raise it and also replace it ...'

Whether the boat *was* launched that way, through an opening in the rails, was never specifically surmised in the court proceedings, much less ascertained. Charles Edey Fay, however, was less circumspect:

> It seems probable that the rails mentioned had been removed by her crew in order to launch her boat over the side. There were no remains of a painter [boat's bow-line] or boat-rope fastened to the rail.[3]

OPEN HATCHES AND SKYLIGHT

There were two hatches on the *Mary Celeste* leading to areas below her main deck, and a small hatch at her stern: one at the bow, the *fore hatch*, leading to the forepart of her hold; one in the centre of the ship, the *main hatch*, leading directly down into the cargo hold; and the *lazarette*, at the stern, a small compartment for provisions, spare ropes, paint and the like.

Deveau and Wright found the fore hatch and lazarette open when they boarded the derelict. The hatch covers, right side up, were lying on the deck by the side of the hatches. Why the hatches were open at all, and whether the covers were upside down or right side up on the deck, became details of some controversy in later *Mary Celeste* chronicles.

The open fore hatch *might* have been a clue about *why* the *Mary Celeste* was abandoned. The open lazarette hatch at the stern *might* have been a clue about the *manner* of her abandonment.

Mate Deveau testified that the skylight in the roof of the master's cabin, which was elevated to a height of a few feet above the main deck, 'was open and raised', which would have allowed any spray or seawater or rain to get through and wet the cabin. Second mate Wright, however, testified that 'the sky light was in a good state – it was not open'. Charles Lund, who went on the *Mary Celeste* to Gibraltar, testified that when he first went on board her, 'The sky light was open ...'

On balance, then, the *Mary Celeste*'s cabin skylight was probably open, and, so, probably a source of water that contributed to the wet conditions they all found below deck.

BINNACLE

The binnacle is a pedestal on the top of which a compass, half-hooded in a metal (often brass) housing, is fixed on the deck in front of the steering wheel for the helmsman to steer a compass course. It is usually bolted to the deck. The compass itself has a glass case and a light (by oil lamp before electric lights were introduced) for the helmsman to see the compass points and ship's course at night.

The binnacle on the *Mary Celeste* was wooden. It was attached to the roof of the main cabin by lines lashed to cleats, which are like double-winged metal hooks. All the men who first boarded the *Mary Celeste* remarked on it being knocked over and lying on the deck by the steering wheel, which, they all noted, was loose and swinging freely. According to Deveau:

> 'The binnacle was injured [damaged] when I went on board. I fixed it and used it on our way here [Gibraltar]. The glass was broken. The binnacle was washed away from its place and I set it back again. It is lashed on the top of the cabin above the deck; being a wooden one, the lashings had given way – one of the cleats was gone.'

The binnacle might have been knocked over by a sea coming on board the *Mary Celeste* after she was deserted. Or it might, conceivably, have been knocked astray by the hurried launching of a boat by men desperate to get off the ship. *Dei Gratia* men speaking to the court intimated the possibility of the former; none suggested any likelihood of the latter.

Below Deck

THE GALLEY AND 'HOT FOOD'

When Oliver Deveau went into the main cabin of the *Mary Celeste*, meaning Capt. Briggs' cabin, he 'saw no preparation made for eating in the Cabin. There was plenty to eat, but all the knives and forks were in the pantry … There was nothing to eat or drink in the cabin on the table, but preserved meats in the pantry.'

As for the galley, which he said was awash with water 'a foot or so deep':

> 'I examined the state of the ship's galley … and all the things, pots & kettle etc. were washed up … there were no cooked provisions in the galley … she had I should say six months provisions on board.'

Second mate John Wright testified that:

> '… the stove [in the galley] was knocked out of its place, that could have been done by a sea striking the galley and the stove through the door, it would knock the stove out of its place …'

Charles Edey Fay, doyen of *Mary Celeste* chroniclers, has noted that the galley:

> … was in a bad state, with a great deal of water … The viands on a still-hot stove – so graphically described by the romanticists – were conspicuous by their absence, for the stove had been knocked out of place and there was no heat in it or food on it …

To a generation which has been entertained by imaginative writers with minute descriptions of 'a freshly cooked breakfast' with 'three cups of tea – lukewarm – oatmeal, coffee, bacon and eggs' on the cabin table, it will come as a surprise to learn the dry facts from First Mate Deveau's testimony ...[4]

So, contrary to the popular iteration by later chroniclers, fablers and fabulists, that everyone had scampered off the ship a few hours before, leaving their hot 'viands' and cups of warm tea behind and the galley stove warm with recent use, the truth was rather more frugal.

IN THE CABINS

On his first and second appearances before the court, on 18 and 20 December, mate Deveau spoke about the state in which he found Capt. Briggs' and the mates' cabins, and the crew's accommodation in their forecastle (or *fo'c's'le*, as sailors always call it), as he prowled around under deck:

18 December: 'I found everything wet in the [captain's] cabin in which there had been a great deal of water ... I found all the Captain's effects had been left. I mean his clothing, furniture &c. The bed was just as they had left it. The bed and other clothes were wet. I judged that there had been a woman on board [by the nature of some of the clothing in the cabin] ...

'I found the log book in the mate's cabin on his desk, the log slate I found on the [captain's] cabin table. I found an entry in the log book up to the 24th November and an entry on the log slate dated 25th November showing that they had made the Island of Saint Mary [Santa Maria] ...

'There seemed to be everything left behind in the cabin as if left in a great hurry but everything in its place. I noticed the impression in the Captain's bed as of a child having lain there.'

20 *December*: 'I have said that there was the appearance on the bed in the Captain's Cabin as if a child had slept in it. There was room in

berth for a child and a woman and also for the Captain. I saw articles of Child's wearing apparel, also Child's toys. The bed was as it had been left, being slept in, not made.'

The rest of his testimony about the state of the cabin was to the effect that there was a variety of male and female clothing in boxes and drawers and under the bed, some of which were wet or damp, as was the bedding, and some not. The windows around the cabin were 'battened up' with canvas and boards. He surmised that water might have got through the open skylight.

The most telling evidence of the haste with which the *Mary Celeste* was deserted was as Deveau noted:

'The men's clothing [in the fo'c's'le] was all left behind, their oilskin boots and even their pipes, as if they had left in a great hurry or haste. My reason for saying that they left in haste is that a sailor would generally take such things, especially his pipe, if not in great haste ...

'The Chronometer, the Sextant and Navigation book were all absent, the ship's register and papers also not found.'

And: 'There was a harmonium or melodium in the cabin', which was apparently in a perfectly good condition.

As for the state of the cargo of barrels of alcohol in the hold, and evidence of any grog elsewhere in the ship:

'... the cargo seemed to be in good condition and well stowed and had not shifted, as far as I could judge the cargo was not injured. I found no wine, beer or spirits whatever in the ship.'

'LETTER TO FANNIE' AND THE 'MYSTERY CAT'

What was *not* found in any of the under-deck cabins, by any of the court testifiers, was a 'Dear Fannie ...' letter supposedly started but left hurriedly unwritten by the *Mary Celeste*'s first mate Albert Richardson to his wife Frances, and 'found' on a table in one of the cabins.

What *was* found, at least as testified by Capt. Winchester after he arrived in Gibraltar and appeared in court on 29 January 1873, was an inscription on the *Mary Celeste* log slate:

> 'I do not think that any of the entries written in upon this slate are in [mate] Richardson's handwriting, except the last line on the left hand side engraved or scratched on the Slate "Frances my own dear wife Frances N.R."'

'N.R.' were initials of Richardson's wife, Frances (Fannie) N. Richardson. Whether the scratchings on a slate constituted a hurriedly engraved start of a 'letter' to his wife, or were simply a fond reminiscence about the mate's wife whom he missed, this brief inscription made its way into a number of later *Mary Celeste* myth-stories.

Nor was there a cat, or any signs whatsoever of a feline presence having been on board during the *Mary Celeste*'s voyage. Both the letter and the moggie materialised later from the vapours of creative fictionists about the *Mary Celeste* mystery.

The alleged cat (and, for that matter, the 'Dear Fannie ...' letter) was like T.S. Eliot's 'Mystery Cat', Macavity, who could never be found after a crime, to 'the Flying Squad's despair', because, 'when they reach the scene of crime – *Macavity's not there*!'

Mr Solly-Flood's Suspicions

Queen's Proctor Mr Solly-Flood heard 'so extraordinary a picture' of the *Mary Celeste* incident by the testimonies of Deveau, Wright, Lund, Anderson and Johnson, up to 22 December 1872, that he was aroused to suspect that there might have been more nefarious acts in play that caused the abandonment of the vessel. So inflamed were the suspicions of Mr Solly-Flood that, on 23 December, he ordered that an exhaustive inspection of her, inside and out, and around her hull, be conducted.

This was carried out the same day by John Austin, a marine surveyor at Gibraltar, and Ricardo Portunato, a diver. Thomas Joseph Vecchio, Marshal of the Court, boarded the *Mary Celeste* with them and Queen's Proctor Solly-Flood.

The results of that survey, together with a further 'more minute examination [of the ship] for marks of violence', conducted on 7 January 1873, were like the strain of a virus impregnated into Mr Solly-Flood's fevered imagination about the most likely violent cause of, and 'solution' to, the *Mary Celeste*'s derelict condition.

At around this time, on 23 December, the *Dei Gratia* sailed for Genoa, where she arrived on 16 January 1873 to deliver her cargo of petroleum. Capt. Morehouse had put the ship under the command of mate Deveau. Capt. Morehouse himself stayed behind in Gibraltar as the representative of the owners in the salvage hearings. Judge Cochrane was not a little miffed by the vessel's departure:

> 'The conduct of the Salvors in going away, as they have done, has, in my opinion, been most reprehensible and may probably influence the decision as to their claim for remuneration for their services [i.e., a salvage reward], and it appears very strange why the Captain of the *Dei Gratia* who knows little or nothing to help the investigation, should have remained here, whilst the First Mate and the crew who boarded the *Celeste* and brought her here should have been allowed to go away as they have done.'

Dei Gratia, it should be remembered, had been held up at Gibraltar for eleven days, since 12 December. She was running up costs. A delay in delivering her cargo would almost certainly incur penalty charges. And she had another consignment scheduled for her to pick up at Messina. There was some urgency, therefore, to get her on her way from Gibraltar. Capt. Morehouse would still be there to help with the court's enquiries. Oliver Deveau himself was later recalled from Genoa to be cross-examined for a third time in the court, on 4 March 1873.

Capt. Winchester Arrives in Gibraltar

Meanwhile, amidst the incipient rumblings in the mind of Mr Solly-Flood about possible devilry afoot in the *Mary Celeste* case, the ship's principal owner, Capt. Winchester, arrived in Gibraltar to oversee his interests. His appearance stemmed from a telegram he received at his New York office on 14 December that 'Brig *Mary Celeste* found 4th [December] brought to Gibraltar'. On Christmas day 1872 he took passage on a steamship to Liverpool and from there went on to Gibraltar, arriving on 15 January 1873.

On 20 January the US Consul at Gibraltar, Mr Horatio Sprague, wrote to the US Department of State (now the State Department) of Capt. Winchester's arrival:

> I have now to inform you that [*Mary Celeste*'s] principal owner, Mr James H. Winchester, arrived here on the 15th instant from New York for the purpose of claiming the Brig and attending to the interests of all those concerned in her case ...
>
> ... in the meanwhile, nothing is heard from the missing crew of the *Mary Celeste*, and in face of the apparently seaworthy condition of this vessel, it is difficult to account for her abandonment, particularly as her Master, who was well-known, bore the highest character for seamanship and correctness ...
>
> The Queen's Proctor in the Vice Admiralty Court, of this City, who is also the Attorney General, seems to take the greatest interest in the case and rather entertains the apprehension of some foul play having occurred ... – ... so far the matter is wrapped up in mystery.

Mr Solly-Flood's Survey

The survey of the *Mary Celeste* on 23 December 1872 and overseen by Surveyor John Austin comprised a comprehensive examination of the ship as found in the Bay of Gibraltar. It is important to note that it was carried out two and a half weeks after the *Dei Gratia* had found her derelict on the high seas, after she had been made shipshape for her run to Gibraltar, and ten days after her actual arrival at Gibraltar.

The *Mary Celeste*'s condition at the time of the survey was therefore in many ways very different from how she was found as a derelict. Nevertheless, amongst the more notable points of the survey were the following.

THE SPLINTERED BOWS AND A BLOODY SWORD

The *bow* area of a ship, at the pointy end, is at the opposite end of her *stern*, the (usually, but not always) blunt or square end. The *bows* of a ship are the two sides of her, including gunwale and rails, to the right (*starboard bow*) and left (*port bow*) of the pointy-most point of her bow.

Kate Winslet and Leonardo DiCaprio stood on the rails at the *bow* of the *Titanic* with their arms wings-spanned over her *port* and *starboard bows*. They jumped off her stern as *Titanic* dove head-first – *bow-down* – into the deep.

The report of Surveyor Austin's inspection of the *Mary Celeste* noted that he found on the port bow of the vessel 'between two and three feet above the water line', cuts to her planking which were:

> to the depth of about three eighths of an inch or about one inch and a quarter wide for a length of about 6 or 7 feet. This injury had been sustained very recently and could not have been effected by the weather and was apparently done by a sharp cutting instrument continuously applied thro' the whole length of the injury.

Austin reported a similar 'injury' on the starboard bow.

What he was stating was that some of the wood planking around both of the *Mary Celeste*'s bows was splintered. What he was inferring was that this was deliberate, 'done by a sharp cutting instrument'. And what that implied, but perhaps only to Mr Solly-Flood's flaring imagination, was some manner of foul play.

None of the *Dei Gratia* crew who first or even subsequently went on board the *Mary Celeste* found anything damaged around her bows that might arouse suspicions of 'injury' inflicted there. Capt. Morehouse testified that, on the day the *Dei Gratia* encountered the derelict, through his telescope from a distance he 'saw the marks or spalls on the bows of the *Mary Celeste*'. He otherwise found nothing particularly remarkable to add to that observation.

Amongst numerous other observations Austin made in the survey was that he found, 'on a little bracket', or shelf, in the mate's cabin:

> a small phial of oil for a sewing machine in its proper perpendicular position, a reel of cotton for such a machine, and a thimble. If they had been there in bad weather then they would have been thrown down or carried away.

The phial of sewing machine oil became a small but oft-repeated icon of *Mary Celeste* historiography. Later narratives placed its 'perpendicular position' on various surfaces, such as a table in the captain's cabin. This supposedly suggested that the ship had not weathered stormy conditions before the *Dei Gratia* found her; not stormy enough, by implication, to cause her to be abandoned.

But not one of the *Dei Gratia* men in their court testimonies mentioned this article, or a thimble, on a table or bracket or anywhere else (apart from mate Deveau's observation of various sewing paraphernalia in a bag in the captain's cabin). They only emerged in Austin's survey after the *Mary Celeste* had arrived at Gibraltar. And, whether she might have experienced stormy weather in the open Atlantic, she certainly had in the Straits of Gibraltar.

Sailors were traditionally wont to put a vessel in good order before arriving in port. It is more than likely that the *Dei Gratia* salvors, in tidying up the *Mary Celeste*, placed these articles on some flat surface soon before or just after the *Mary Celeste* anchored in the Bay of Gibraltar. They were, most likely, indicative of nothing more mysterious than sailors' habitual good housekeeping.

How the 'small phial of oil for a sewing machine' remained 'perpendicular' on a shelf, even in the relative calm of the Bay of Gibraltar but still subject to the occasional unsteadying influences of winter weather thereabouts, is a bit of a conundrum in itself.

More significant, in the subsequent suppositions of violence afoot on the *Mary Celeste*, was a sword in Capt. Briggs' cabin:

> I also observed in this cabin a Sword in its scabbard which the Marshall [Thomas Vecchio, Marshal of the Court] informed me he had noticed when he came on board for the purpose of arresting the vessel. It had not [been] affected by water but on drawing out the blade it appeared to me as if it had been smeared with blood and afterwards wiped.

And towards the end of the report:

> I found no wine or beer or spirits on board … & did not discover the slightest trace of there having been any explosion or any fire or of anything calculated to create an alarm of an explosion or fire.
>
> … I am wholly unable to discover any reason whatever why the said Vessel should have been abandoned.

A bloody sword and deliberately inflicted 'injury' to the *Mary Celeste*'s bows was, nevertheless, more than enough kindling to stoke Mr Solly-Flood's suspicions. On 22 January 1873, he wrote to the Marine Department of the Board of Trade in London, to keep them abreast of the case. In that letter he informed the Board that the 'deliberate' cuts to the bows and the 'bloody' sword (which 'appeared to me to exhibit traces of blood and to have been wiped clean') were grounds to conduct 'a still more minute examination for marks of violence'.

That inspection had been held two weeks before, on 7 January, when Mr Solly-Flood was accompanied by five Royal Naval officers and Marshal Vecchio, 'all of whom agreed with me in opinion that the injury to the bows had been effected intentionally by a sharp instrument'. The very first observation made in the visit by the seven men, recorded in Mr Solly-Flood's report, was:

> On examining the Starboard top-gallant rail, marks were discovered apparently of blood and a mark of a blow apparently of a sharp axe.

This letter became infamous not only for the apparent confirmation of Mr Solly-Flood's suspicions by the discovery of apparent signs of violence, but even more for his concluding remarks:

> My object is to move the Bd. Of Trade to take such action as they may think fit to discover if possible the fate of the Master, his wife and child, and the crew of the derelict.

And then the conjecture which the Queen's Proctor advanced and became a pillar of subsequent *Mary Celeste* narratives:

> My own theory or guess is that the Crew got at the alcohol and in the fury of drunkenness murdered the Master whose name was Briggs and wife and Child and the Chief Mate – that they then damaged the bows of the Vessel with the view of giving it the appearance of having struck on rocks or suffered from a collision so as to induce the Master of any Vessel wh. might pick them up if they saw her at some distance to think her not worth attempting to save and that they did sometime between the 25th Novbr. and the 5th Decbr. escape on board some vessel bound for some north or South American port or the West Indies.

So, that was it: the *Mary Celeste* was, for the Queen's Proctor, a case of mass murder on the high seas, committed by the second mate and the rest of her crew, who got blind drunk by breaking into and debauching themselves from the cargo of toxic denatured alcohol, and jumped a damaged and therefore most likely unsalvageable ship, in the hope of being picked up by a passing vessel headed west to a port somewhere, anywhere, in that general direction.

And that, despite no evidence found by any of the *Dei Gratia* men or the more forensic investigation by Surveyor Austin that any of the 1,701 barrels of alcohol on the *Mary Celeste* had been tampered with, much less breached. Mate Deveau, an observant and experienced seaman, had already remarked in his first testimony to the court that when he first boarded the *Mary Celeste*, 'the cargo seemed to be in good condition and well stowed and had not shifted, as far as I could judge the cargo was not injured'.

The Mystery of the Missing 'Blood Report'

Mr Solly-Flood was now in the heat of the chase to pin down his suspicions as fact – Truth! – and pursued his notions of foul play. He ordered 'a careful and minute inspection of the vessel' by a certain Dr J. Patron. The examination would be 'for the purpose', Dr Patron noted in his report of 30 January, 'of ascertaining whether any marks or stains of blood could be discovered on or in her hulk'. That included the 'blood' stains on the sword which, he remarked, were 'of a more suspicious character'.

Dr Patron meticulously tested all the apparent blood stains on the deck of the *Mary Celeste*, and from the sword. All his results came up negative:

> From the preceding negative experiments I feel myself authorized to conclude that according to our present scientifical knowledge there is no blood either in the stains observed on the deck of the *Mary Celeste* or on those found on the blade of the sword that I have examined.

The blood report was presented to the court 'under seal' on 14 March 1873. And it remained so sealed, lodged in Attorney General Solly-Flood's office, and the contents undisclosed, for fourteen years.

Consul Sprague had a particular interest in knowing of any evidence pointing to any violence that might have occurred on an American vessel. He was 'confidentially informed' that the judge of the court, Sir James Cochrane, refused to allow any knowledge of Dr Patron's findings to be revealed. Everyone connected with the *Mary Celeste* case, though, apparently knew about the negative blood results at the time.

So what was the reason for such secrecy?

Mr Solly-Flood himself remained silent on the reason for twelve years. In a byzantine-worded and voluminous letter he wrote to Consul Sprague, who was still in office, dated 9 January 1885 (in which he composed a single, uninterrupted and virtually unintelligible sentence of 223 words!), Mr Solly-Flood explained that he was convinced that the perpetrators of what he still insisted had been violence aboard the *Mary Celeste* were alive and hiding out somewhere. Keeping them ignorant of the evidence in the court proceedings would somehow allow them to think they had got away with their criminality. That, he wrote, would flush them out, thinking 'they could safely emerge from concealment', which 'would probably reveal the mystery on which the fate of all who sailed in the vessel and the cause of her abandonment were involved'.

How and why the alleged villains might offer such a self-incriminating solution to the mystery was not revealed by Mr Solly-Flood and remained 'under seal' for ever within the confines of his febrile imagination. Needless to say, none of his phantom miscreants ever materialised.

Consul Sprague wrote a letter to the Assistant Secretary of State in response to Mr Solly-Flood's 1885 letter, repudiating most of his allegations and so-called reasonings. He spared nothing in his opinion of the man:

> In conclusion, I would beg to state confidentially, that Mr. Flood is an Irish gentleman. Although reported as being over eighty years of age, has always been considered an individual of very vivid

> imagination, and to have survived, to some extent at least, the judicious application of his mental faculties; such is, I believe, the general opinion of the community at large, even among his most intimate and personal friends.

The seal on Dr Patron's 'blood report' of 30 January 1873 was finally broken by the Court Registrar fourteen years later, in July 1887. A copy was handed to Consul Sprague, who then sent it to his Department of State on 29 July 1887.

Consul Sprague's Survey

Rewinding back to the events of 1873, early in February of that auspicious year Consul Sprague updated his Department of State superiors on the status of the blood survey from a week before, 'the result of which is considered to negative anything like blood existing thereon'. He had requested from a visiting US Navy commander, Capt. Shufeldt, of the USS *Plymouth*, which arrived at Gibraltar on 5 February from Villefranche on her way home via Lisbon, that he look over the *Mary Celeste* for any indications of violence that had been cited in the earlier surveys, and her general condition.

Capt. Shufeldt's conclusion was, 'after a cursory examination of the vessel and a somewhat imperfect knowledge of the circumstances' on 6 February:

> I am of the opinion that she was abandoned by the master & crew in a moment of panic & for no sufficient reason. She may have strained in the gale through which she was passing & for the time leaked so much as to alarm the Master, and it is possible that, at this moment, another vessel in sight, induced him (having his wife and child on board,) to abandon thus hastily. In this event, he may not be heard from for some time to come, as the ship which rescued him may have been bound to a distant port.

> I reject the idea of mutiny, from the fact that there is no evidence of violence about the decks or in the cabins ... The damage about the bows of the Brig appears to me to amount to nothing more than splinters made in the bending of the planks – which were afterwards forced off by the action of the sea ... nor by any possible chance, the result of an intention to do so.
>
> The vessel at the present moment appears staunch and seaworthy – Some day, I hope & expect to hear from her crew. If surviving, the Master will regret his hasty action. But if we should never hear of them again, I shall nevertheless think they were lost in the boat in which both Master & crew abandoned the Mary Celeste & shall remember with interest this sad and silent mystery of the sea.

Capt. Oliver Briggs and the Julia A. Hallock

During the farrago of inquiry hearings at Gibraltar, Capt. Oliver Briggs, brother of the missing Capt. Benjamin, was taking his own vessel, the *Julia A. Hallock*, from Gijón in north-west Spain to Messina, in southern Italy. He and Benjamin had planned to meet at Messina some time in February 1873 when the *Mary Celeste* was scheduled to pick up a cargo there. The sea, however, once again took its toll. Neither of the Briggs brothers, as it turned out, would be spared that tariff.

The *Hallock* left Gijón on 6 January 1873. A few days later, a Bay of Biscay gale 'blew fearfully'. The ship began to leak:

> On the 8th a tremendous sea struck the vessel, and, as she was flying light [i.e., with no cargo], she capsized. The captain and crew succeeded in getting on her side, but were soon washed off, and one man was drowned. The others got back, but were repeatedly washed off, and all were drowned except Mr. Perry [second officer] and a seaman named Kenney, who got on the ship's house ['an enclosed

> structure built on the top deck of a vessel'], which had become separated from the vessel, after she went down.
>
> Mr. Perry was on the house for nearly five days, and suffered much from want of water. On the 10th Kenney, who suffered very much from exhaustion, caused by cold and hunger, died, and his body was committed to the sea. On the morning of Monday, the 13th, the brig *Prosperous*, of Sunderland, Capt. William Shotton, bound from the Tyne [north-east England] for Oporto, fell in with Mr. Perry, and took him off the poophouse. He had drifted during the five days he was on the wreck upwards of 140 miles to the east-north-east.
>
> Among those who drowned were: the Captain, Oliver A. Briggs, master; ...[5]

Mrs Sophia Briggs had now lost all five of her seafaring children. James, her only surviving child, became a businessman at New Bedford and died in 1922. Sophia Matilda Cobb Briggs died at Marion on 5 March 1889, aged 85. Other members of the Cobb-Briggs clan would later continue to pursue the truth, one way or another, about the mysterious case of the *Mary Celeste*.

Capt. Winchester: In Court – then in Spain – then Home

The *Mary Celeste*'s main owner, Capt. James Winchester, had been knocking around Gibraltar for two weeks after he arrived from New York on 15 January 1873, to look after his interests in the case. He was finally called to give evidence at the court hearings on 29 January.

Capt. Winchester confirmed that the ship's cargo 'consisted of 1701 barrels of alcohol' and that 'to my knowledge she had no other cargo'. He also said that 'Captain B. Briggs bore a high character, the character of a courageous officer and good seaman who would not, I think, desert his ship except to save his life.' He paid similar testimony to the quality of 'Mate Richardson'; and the seven *Mary Celeste* crew members, amongst other details.

As for the sword, bloodied or otherwise, and the splintered bows:

> 'I do not know anything of the Captain or Mate having a sword nor of a sword being on board at all. I never saw such a sword ... I do not know whether either of them carried a revolver or gun which would be a much more likely weapon for them to have ...
>
> 'My explanation of the long splints or marks in her bow is that they spauled [splintered] off the wood having been steamed and bent to fit it on.'

His concluding remarks to Queen's Advocate Solly-Flood's cross-examination confirmed his belief in the 'high character' and impeccable seamanship of the *Mary Celeste*'s master, officers and crew:

> 'From what I have seen of the state and condition of the vessel I cannot believe she was abandoned by her Master, Officers and crew in consequence of stress of weather only. I had plenty of time to examine her thoroughly and feel very certain that she was not abandoned through perils of sea ...
>
> 'I am very certain both men [Capt. Briggs and Mate Richardson] would remain by their ship to the last and that neither would have deserted the ship unless forced to do so or in fear of their lives.'

In the first week of February, after his court appearance, Capt. Winchester crossed into Spain to go to Cadiz, just up the coast from Gibraltar. There he expected to find an old ship-broker acquaintance, possibly to get moral, technical or financial support, or all three, to aid in the pursuit of his claim in the *Mary Celeste* case. That acquaintance, he discovered, had died.

But every cloud ... He encountered a family friend, a young shipmaster, Capt. Henry Appleby, of the brigantine *Daisy Boynton*, who had recently delivered a cargo to Cadiz and 'received [the *Daisy Boynton*'s] freight money'. Capt. Winchester needed funds to pay for the running costs of keeping his ship at Gibraltar. Young Capt. Appleby loaned him the freight money and took an IOU note for it.

Capt. Winchester, however, learned soon after that in New York his ailing wife's health was deteriorating. His business there was also, he believed, suffering from his absence. So, from Cadiz he went to Lisbon to take a steamship home, where he arrived on 25 February 1873.

Final Court Appearances

The final hearings at the Vice-Admiralty Court were held from 3 to 5 March 1873. By far the greater part of the proceedings was taken up by the testimonies of the *Dei Gratia* master Capt. Morehouse, who had been in Gibraltar since 12 December, and mate Oliver Deveau, who had been recalled from Genoa where the *Dei Gratia* had arrived on 16 January.

PORT AND STARBOARD TACK

Capt. Morehouse's most telling testimony was that, when he first sighted the *Mary Celeste*:

> 'We were on the port tack, she was on the starboard tack.'

This was not in itself startling news. Other *Dei Gratia* crew members mate Deveau and seaman Charles Lund had already voiced the same observation to the court. But the fact of *Mary Celeste* being on starboard tack, heading in the opposite direction to the *Dei Gratia* on port tack, was of some significance to the mystery of her abandonment.

What port and starboard tack meant, as far as the *Dei Gratia* and *Mary Celeste* were concerned on the day of their encounter, was that the northerly wind at that time and place was blowing over the *port* (left-hand) side of the *Dei Gratia* heading *east*, and therefore on port tack.

It was blowing over the *starboard* (right-hand) side of the *Mary Celeste* heading *west*, so she was on starboard tack.

Mate Deveau remarked as much in his testimony:

> 'She was sheeted on the starboard tack when we found her.'

Dei Gratia had recorded no change in the northerly wind direction she experienced between 25 November and 4 December when she encountered the derelict; she was on port tack all that time.

But the log slate of the *Mary Celeste* recorded that, on 25 November, just as she was passing to the south and through the Azores, she was in fact experiencing westerly winds. A local west wind south of the islands would have caused the *Mary Celeste*, on a course heading just south of due east, to be on starboard tack.

At that same time, though, the *Dei Gratia* was a week behind the *Mary Celeste* and a thousand or so miles still to the west in the mid-Atlantic. She only reached the Azores, sailing around 200 miles north of the islands, at the beginning of December. By the time she came across the derelict *Mary Celeste* on 4 December, it's likely that the northerly wind direction would have been different from the local westerly winds that the *Mary Celeste* had experienced on the southern fringes of the islands a week earlier.

One thing was clear: the *Mary Celeste*, at some time and somewhere after she passed Santa Maria on 25 November, swung around to head west. Her steering wheel was loose when the *Dei Gratia* found her; any change in wind direction would have allowed her to swing around freely to head in a different direction – including back towards the west.

The point is that, whenever and wherever the *Mary Celeste* ran into the constant northerly winds the *Dei Gratia* described, there was by then no one on board her to reset her sails from starboard to port tack to keep her on her course eastwards towards the Straits of Gibraltar. The ship was by then devoid of all her ten souls – a ghost ship, her course dictated not by any human presence but by the whim of the North Atlantic breezes.

Abandoned, with the set of her sails still on starboard tack, she would have been swung round by a northerly wind shift to head roughly west, veering about a generally westerly direction.

Which is precisely how the *Dei Gratia* found her.

The question was, when and how far *east* had she travelled since 25 November before everyone on board jumped ship, and then, with a change in wind direction, she turned *west*, to be found derelict and still on starboard tack on 4 December by the *Dei Gratia* salvors?

She could only have been abandoned after 25 November when mate Richardson (or possibly Capt. Briggs) made that final log slate note, the last date indicating people were still on board her. The general assumption was that everyone left her in a panic very soon after that 8 a.m. position of 25 November just to the north of the island of Santa Maria. Otherwise there would almost certainly have been a later log slate entry than the one of that morning.

But that was only an assumption; an educated guess, no doubt, by people who understood such things, but not a fact – certainly not 'The Truth'.

Whenever and *wherever* the *Mary Celeste* was abandoned while she remained on starboard tack, as well as *why* and *how* the ten souls on board deserted her, conjoined to constitute what became 'The Greatest Sea Mystery'.

Mate Deveau

Mate Oliver Deveau was the last person to testify at the Vice-Admiralty Court, on Tuesday, 4 March 1873. Some of the salient points of his statements included the absence of any remnants of a boat's bow rope, or painter, 'fastened to the rail' or otherwise which might have indicated where and how (and if) the *Mary Celeste* crew had launched a getaway boat. He also observed the absence of 'any mark of an axe on the rail or cut ... I can form no opinion about the cause of the axe cut on the rail' mentioned in Mr Solly-Flood's 'minute examination' of the *Mary Celeste* on 7 January. Finally, there was an absence of 'marks or traces of blood upon the deck', though he could not 'say whether there were any or not', which, like the axe cuts, might have indicated some violence on board.

Deveau did find the sword which the Marshall of the Court, Thomas Vecchio, had noticed when he went on board to arrest the *Mary Celeste* almost three months before, and which appeared in Surveyor Austin's report 'as if it had been smeared with blood and afterwards wiped'. Deveau, however, was singularly unimpressed with the putative instrument of a violent assault on board the ship:

> 'I saw a sword on board the *Mary Celeste*. I found that sword under the Captain's berth. I took it out from there. I looked at it, drew it from its sheath, there was nothing remarkable on it. I do not think there is anything remarkable about it now; it seems rusty.'

He also noted that he found Mrs Briggs' sewing machine 'in the cabin, under the sofa, certainly not on the harmonium when we first went on board the *Celeste*; I may have put it there myself as I looked at it …' Where it was *not* was on a table with material under its needle, as if Mrs Briggs had been sewing when she had to hasten away to abandon ship – a standard bit of fiction invented and reiterated in later narratives.

As for his thoughts about why the *Mary Celeste* had been abandoned, and if it was caused by a violent affray of some sort:

> 'It did not occur to me that there had been any act of violence, there was nothing whatever to induce one to believe or to show that there had been any violence. I used often, when at the wheel, to think how and why the vessel had been abandoned by her crew and came to the conclusion that she had been left in panic …
>
> 'She was so sound and stout that I cannot think that if I had been on board I should have abandoned her. I should have considered her safer than an open boat unless she was on the rocks.'

The question left dangling by mate Deveau's opinion of 'panic' rather than violence afoot to cause all ten souls to desert the *Mary Celeste* was, of course: panicked by *what*? After 150 years, that unresolved uncertainty continues to shadow, indeed to epitomise, The Greatest Sea Mystery.

Mary Celeste Sails Again

On 25 February 1873, a few weeks before the Vice-Admiralty Court concluded its sessions, Consul Sprague successfully gained the release of the *Mary Celeste* from her enforced detention at Gibraltar since 13 December 1872, into the hands of her owners. It is interesting to note how the London daily shipping newspaper *Lloyd's List* mis-recorded the vessel's name in its 1 March 1873 edition:

> Gibraltar, 25th Feb.– The *Marie Celeste*, from New York to Genoa, reported, 13th Dec., as having been brought in here, derelict, will proceed to her destination to discharge.

On 7 March, the *Mary Celeste* was cleared to 'proceed to her destination to discharge' and sail to Genoa to deliver her cargo of alcohol under a new master, Capt. George Blatchford, and crew sent out by Capt. Winchester from New York. Having lain at Gibraltar for almost three months, she sailed on 10 March and arrived at Genoa on 21 March. Apart from nine empty barrels, from leakage, her alcohol cargo was intact and 'in excellent condition'.

Salvage Award

On 14 March, a few days after *Mary Celeste*'s departure from Gibraltar, the presiding judge of the court, Sir James Cochrane, delivered his verdict on the salvage reward to be granted the *Dei Gratia* salvors. After almost three months of scrutiny of the evidence, he 'gave judgment in the *Mary Celeste* case, and awarded the sum of £1,700 to the master and crew of the Nova Scotian brigantine *Dei Gratia* for the salvage services rendered by them; the costs of the suit to be paid out of the property salved'.

Judge Cochrane swatted away at the persistent buzz of the bee in his bonnet about Capt. Morehouse allowing a central witness, mate

Oliver Deveau, to leave Gibraltar in the midst of the hearings to take the *Dei Gratia* to Genoa. He 'thought it right to express the disapprobation of the court as to the conduct' of both men. That dereliction, he wrote, 'rendered necessary the analysis of the supposed spots or stains of blood found on the deck of the *Mary Celeste* and on the sword'. The costs of the blood analysis, he decided, 'should be charged against the amount awarded to the salvors'.

Why or how mate Deveau's temporary absence 'rendered necessary the analysis' of the supposed blood marks seems an attenuated thread of logic. Compared, however, with Queen's Proctor Solly-Flood's runaway train of imaginative suppositions, Judge Cochrane's reasoning might seem cogent, if spitefully spurious.

The *Mary Celeste* was worth, it was said at the time, $5,700, and her cargo, $36,943: total, $42,643. The equivalent dollar amount of the salvage award, 'about $8,300', was a bit under 20 per cent of that total. It was acknowledged later by salvage insurance authorities that the payday for the salvors was significantly less than it might, or even should, have been, compared with the risks the *Dei Gratia* master and crew took in bringing the *Mary Celeste* to port.

It was also about half the amount, or even less, relative to the value of the derelict, of other typical salvage rewards around that time. Though it can never be known for sure, the lingering suspicions of Mr Solly-Flood and their contagion of Judge Cochrane's sense of 'disapprobation' might have influenced the frugal remuneration to the *Dei Gratia* salvors.

Last Years of the Mary Celeste

As for the *Mary Celeste* herself, she lay at Genoa from the time she arrived on 21 March 1873 until 26 June when she sailed for Boston, 'the charterers having cancelled her charter-party', presumably for the cargo she was scheduled to pick up at Messina. Her bottom was surveyed at Genoa and 'found in perfect order', though why she spent so long there otherwise is not known. Her voyage from Genoa to Boston took just over two months; she arrived on 1 September. From there, on 13 September, she sailed for New York, arriving on 19 September.

After that the *Mary Celeste* had an apparently ordinary voyaging life, including multiple changes of ownership. Her final days, though, were mired in a murky case of barratry – the wilful wrecking of a vessel – by her master at the time, Capt. Gilman Parker, on the Rochelais Reef near Miragoane, west of Port-au-Prince, Haiti, on 3 January 1885. The charge was that the deliberate wrecking of the *Mary Celeste* was an attempt to defraud insurers by the shippers of her mixed cargo, which they all acknowledged at trial.

But that, though tantalising in conspiracy, intrigue, sabotage and suicide, is another story. *Mary Celeste* was a total loss. Born 1861 at Spencer Island – died 1885 at Rochelais Reef, Haiti.

There never was a resolution to how, why and where she had been abandoned on the Atlantic a dozen years before. And even those perceptions put forward by the first-hand observations of the *Dei Gratia* salvors and the Gibraltar surveyors, and surmised by Mr Frederick Solly-Flood, were, for all their authenticity, riven by uncertainty.

Whatever the real truth of The Greatest Sea Mystery, the ten lost souls of the *Mary Celeste* took it to their (probably) watery grave. With nature's abhorrence of a vacuum, the cavernous void of that 150-year-old enigma has sucked into it a fruitful and often florid narrative of myth, fiction, misinformation and 'fake news'.

PART II

THE MYTH

'Get your facts first, and then you can distort them as much as you please.'

Mark Twain, quoted in Rudyard Kipling, *From Sea to Sea* (1899)

Yarns, Tall Tales and 'Fake News'

Charles Edey Fay was an officer of one of the *Mary Celeste*'s insurers, the Atlantic Mutual Insurance Company, of New York, in the 1930s. Fay began researching the case of the mysterious derelict in the early 1930s, 'to state in orderly fashion the salient facts of the story'. Up till then the Vice-Admiralty Court proceedings from 1872 and 1873 had lain archived and virtually incognito in Gibraltar.

Fay was able to get a partial typewritten transcript of them at the time. They left out, however, Capt. Morehouse's and Capt. Winchester's testimonies. Full transcripts only came to light in the 1960s after Fay wrote about the *Mary Celeste* mystery in the early 1940s and '50s. (Charles Edey Fay died at his retirement home in Florida in 1957.)

In the absence of those first-hand transcripts of events at Gibraltar, most pre-1930s news of and commentaries about the case, including semi-fictitious accounts, derived mainly from reports on the hearings by the *Gibraltar Chronicle*, and shipping news sources such as the *New York Journal of Commerce* and the *Shipping and Mercantile Gazette* of London.

It wasn't the case that the transcripts of the Gibraltar hearings were sealed or access to them officially denied. It was simply that they were filed away in the dusty archives of a rather out-of-the-way part of the world. Until Fay came along, when he was 'making a study of the case in connection with his book *Ninety Years of Marine Insurance*, published in 1932', no one had gone looking for them.

After Fay and later serious research-writers unearthed the transcripts, new myths about the mystery petered out. The known facts were in the public domain for anyone who cared enough to peruse them. But the old myths never got pulped, just recycled. And the mystique of the *Mary Celeste* mystery ensured the perpetuation of 'solutions' for which the Petri dish of the Internet most recently has allowed the cultivation of innumerable options.

So the collection, composition and transmission of the facts of the *Mary Celeste* case before Fay's investigations were from a medley of newspaper and magazine reports and articles. Is it any wonder that errors, misinformation, suppositions and pure fantasy printed in such sources were recycled in a rather disorderly fashion, sauced up by the imagination of journalists, editors and other scribblers?

The 'fake news' cycle was especially accentuated as original newspaper articles were often syndicated to multiple other newspapers and magazines without fact-checking in any meaningful way. The contagion of a 'fake news' virus – or, more accurately, viruses – infected the narrative of the *Mary Celeste* mystery for many decades, with little or no remedial intervention. In particular, the narrative of violence, what might be called the Solly-Flood virus, spread as iterations and mutations long after his death in 1888.

Misleading information and suppositions about what happened to cause the *Mary Celeste*'s abandonment began to percolate and spread through the neural news network even before her case at Gibraltar was wound up. Violence was at the forefront of the story from the very beginning. And Solly-Flood's fingerprint was all over it. Other misinformation, such as that the *Mary Celeste* was 'towed into Gibraltar' by the *Dei Gratia*, was pure and long-perpetuated fiction:

> A Brig's Officers Believed to Have Been Murdered at Sea
> It is now believed that the fine brig *Mary Celeste*, of about 236 tons, commanded by Capt. Benjamin Briggs, of Marion, Mass., was seized by pirates in the latter part of November, and that,

> after murdering the Captain, his wife and child, and officers, the vessel was abandoned near the Western Islands [Azores], where the miscreants are supposed [believed] to have landed.
>
> The brig left New York on the 17th of November for Genoa with a cargo of alcohol, and is said to have had a crew consisting mostly of foreigners. The theory now is, that some of the men probably gained access to the cargo, and were thus stimulated to the desperate deed.
>
> The *Mary Celeste* was fallen in with by the British brig *Dei Gratia*, Capt. Morehouse, who left New York about the middle of November. The hull of the *Celeste* was found in good condition, and safely towed into Gibraltar, where she has since remained. The confusion in which many things were found on board (including ladies' apparel, &c.,) led, with other circumstances, to suspicion of wrong and outrage, which has by no means died out …
>
> The general opinion is that there has been foul play on board, as spots of blood on the blade of a sword, in the [captain's] cabin, and on the rails, with a sharp cut on the wood, indicate force or violence having been used, but how or by whom is the question. Soon after the vessel was picked up, it was considered possible that a collision might have taken place. Had this been the case, and the brig's officers and crew saved, they would have been landed long ere this. We trust that if any of New-England's shipmasters can give any information or hint of strange boats or seamen landing at any of the islands [i.e., in the Caribbean or nearby] during the past ninety days, that they will see the importance thereof.[6]

That 'general opinion' of foul play was seeded by the fervid imagination of Mr Solly-Flood. But it was a seed that germinated, budded, and subsequently blossomed for decades. The insinuation appeared around the same time in numerous newspaper reports. One, headlined 'A Mystery From The Sea', was written seemingly by the hand of a news reporter with a predilection for crime fiction, though that might well have been said of many others.

> It is inferred that the crew mutinied and over-powered the officers, killing them or taking them prisoners. They were probably surprised, and quietly gagged and bound. A sword was found that seemed to have been stained with blood, and the fore-topgallant sail was cut as with some sharp instrument, perhaps in a struggle with the man on the lookout, as they must have been near land.[7]

Capt. Shufeldt's opinion, after his examination of the *Mary Celeste* on 6 February 1873, wholly contradicted the notion of violence, as recorded in the *Nautical Gazette*, of New York, in its 29 March 1873 issue, repeating what the commander himself stated at the time:

> Capt. Shufeldt ... altogether rejects the idea of piracy or mutiny, as he could discover no marks of violence about the decks or cabins.

Mary Celeste's owner, Capt. Winchester, clarified the origin of the sword found on the ship in an interview with a New York newspaper in March 1873:

> There has been much said about a bloody sword having been found on board the vessel when she was picked up, and an intimation has been made that a mutiny occurred on the vessel ...
>
> The sword found on board proved to belong to the captain, who got it years ago in Messina, Italy, with a spot of rust upon it. This I learn from Mr. Simpson Hart, of New Bedford, who represents the one-third interest in the vessel, which the Captain, Ben. S. Briggs, of Marion, Mass., holds. [Mr Hart, 'it is believed', loaned Capt. Briggs money to buy his stake in the *Mary Celeste* and thereby 'presumably' acquired an interest in her as mortgagee.][8]

Dr Oliver Cobb, a cousin of both Capt. Briggs and his wife Sarah, claimed a different source. In an article published in the February 1940 edition of *Yachting* magazine to offer a solution to the *Mary Celeste* mystery, Dr Cobb wrote that, on one of Capt. Briggs' pre-*Mary Celeste* voyages, with his wife on board: 'they were at Fiume, Austria, where Captain Briggs picked up a sword with the cross of Navarre on the hilt. The sword later appears on board the *Mary Celeste*.'

The piratical attack theory would come up again in the fake news and fiction forums from time to time. But the more persistent suspicions, in the face of no evidence whatsoever, were of a homicidal mutiny by a drunken crew 'consisting mostly of foreigners', which had a distinctly xenophobic tang about it.

An abduction twist on that supposition was aired in the *Gibraltar Chronicle* in March 1873, to the effect that, as an Australian newspaper, the *Evening News* of Sydney, put it in its 12 April edition: 'The theory would seem to be that the crew, or part of them, murdered the captain, ran the vessel towards the Azores, and escaped in the boats, carrying off the lady and child with them.'

Towards the end of March 1873, the Secretary of the US Treasury Department, William Richardson, issued an advisory for information about the *Mary Celeste* incident. It was smudged with the usual stains of errors. It also reeked with the suppositions and suspicions of a mutinous crew of drunken homicidal deserters that Mr Solly-Flood had advanced in his letter to the Board of Trade in London two months before, on 22 January:

> The Fate of the Brigantine *Mary Celeste*
> The following circular relative to the brigantine *Mary Celeste*, found derelict at sea, has been issued from the Treasury Department, directed to Collectors of Customs and others:
>
> You are requested to furnish this department with any information you may be able to obtain affording a clue which may lead to a discovery of all the facts concerning the desertion of a vessel found on the 13th of December last [*sic* – that was the date the *Mary Celeste* arrived at Gibraltar] in latitude 28 20 north [*sic* – 38° 20' N] and longitude 17 51 west [*sic* – 17° 15' W], derelict at sea, and which was towed [*sic*] into the harbor of Gibraltar by the British vessel *Dei Gratia* ...

> The circumstances of the case tend to arouse grave suspicions that the master, his wife and child and perhaps the chief mate were murdered in the fury of drunkenness by the crew, who had evidently gained access to the alcohol with which the vessel was in part [*sic*] laden. It is thought that the vessel was abandoned by the crew between the 25th day of November and the 5th day of December, and that they either perished at sea, or more likely escaped on some vessel bound for some North or South American port or the West India islands ...[9]

Alleged Conspiracy to Defraud

News-hounds have sensitive noses for sniffing out sleaze. The mysterious and Solly-Flood-maligned case of the *Mary Celeste* in the aftermath of the Gibraltar hearings was ripe for the rumour mill of journo-sniffing. One unsavoury pong that emanated in March 1873, just as the *Mary Celeste* was loosing the bonds of her confinement at Gibraltar, concerned the whiff of fraud in her registry. At least they got right, but only once, that she was a brigantine:

> The Abandoned Ship – No Mutiny, but a Scheme to Defraud the Insurance Companies
>
> The stories in regard to the desertion of the brigantine *Mary Celeste* which another ship recently found abandoned in mid-ocean, are not credited in Custom House circles. Mention is made of several suspicious circumstances to show that more selfish motives than the revolting of the sailors and the slaying of their officers might have prompted the abandonment of the vessel.
>
> A SUN reporter was informed that the *Mary Celeste* had been improperly cleared and sailed under false colors [i.e., a false national flag of registry] after going out of this port [New York]. It was charged that deception was resorted to for the purpose of getting her registered as an American vessel. She was built at Parrsboro

> [*sic*], Nova Scotia, in 1861, and formerly sailed under the British flag, better known as the *Amazon*.
>
> In 1870 she took her present name, and was afterward registered as American built. Deputy Surveyor Bell discovered the deception a few months ago, and took measures to seize the brig on her next arrival in port. Contrary to expectations, she failed to appear here, and the Deputy Surveyor threatened that unless she returned to American waters he would have her seized in whatever foreign port she might enter.
>
> Subsequently the brig reappeared at Boston, and she was attached [seized] by the Collector of the Port. She was appraised at $2,600, and was bonded by the owners in that amount. When she sailed hence on her last voyage she was insured at the rate of $16,000, or $13,400 over the Boston appraisement. This discrepancy furnishes a clue upon which the insurance companies will probably act ...[10]

Mary Celeste's owner Capt. Winchester was having none of this 'atrocious falsehood'. His indignant hackles well and truly raised, he was quick to respond to the scurrilous allegation by the populist New York newspaper, renowned as a pioneer in crime reporting for a mass-market readership:

> Having read an article in the *Sun* of the 12th [March] headed 'The Abandoned Ship,' and setting forth that the brig *Mary Celeste* was not properly cleared at the Custom House when she sailed on her last voyage, and that she sailed under false colors, this is an atrocious falsehood, as the records of the Custom House will show, and we are informed that the Custom House circles mentioned in that article is one Mr. Abeel, a Deputy Surveyor.
>
> We now propose to give the true history of this vessel, as far as we know, together with Mr. Abeel's connection with said vessel. The brig *Mary Celeste* ... in November 1868 arrived at this port a wreck and was sold at public auction by Messrs. Burdett & Denniss to Richard W. Haines, who repaired the vessel by putting in new keel, stern, sternpost,

bottom, and mostly new spars, rigging, sails, &c., at an expense of over $10,000, and, believing he was entitled to put his vessel under the American flag, he at that time applied, through a Customs House broker, for an American register, and obtained it in October, 1869.

Ten months after she had received her register, she was again sold at auction for debt and bought by her present owners, who ran her until April, 1872, without knowing there was any trouble with her register; but at this time the aforesaid Abeel came to our office and stated that the *Mary Celeste* had a fraudulent register.

We told him we were not aware of it. He said it was the case, and, after considerable talk and quibbling, he said he knew we were innocent parties and did not want to be hard on us, and that we could settle the matter. This looked so much like blackmail that Mr. Winchester told him that if the vessel belonged to the United States government they would have to take her, as we had no money to settle with him or anybody else. He then 'sloped.'

We then telegraphed the captain at St. Thomas [Virgin Islands] to take the best freight he could and bring the vessel home, knowing that she would be seized. The brig came to Boston, was there seized on account of her register, appraised by parties appointed by the government and bonded for $2,600, which suit is still pending.

She went from Boston to Cow Bay [Cape Breton Island] and back to New York, and was then torn down to her copper and re-built and made a double-decked vessel, at an expense of $11,500. She then loaded on her present unfortunate voyage, and when she sailed from New York was insured for $14,000, valued at $16,000; and we now would ask if an attempt has been made to defraud the underwriters?

What has become of the captain, his wife and child, officers and crew?[11]

The *Sun* newspaper which printed the original 'atrocious falsehood' had got the bit between its teeth. On 28 March 1873 it published an article sub-headed 'Was the *Mary Celeste* Deserted by her Officers and Crew to Obtain Salvage?':

> The deeper the Custom House authorities enter into the investigation of the mystery surrounding the fate of the officers and crew of the brig *Mary Celeste*, found abandoned within 200 miles of the Spanish coast, the more thoroughly convinced they are that the missing men are alive and safe. It is thought that they voluntarily deserted the vessel for purposes of gain, and that they landed in a small boat on one of the Azores, where they could hide until the interest in their fate had died away. The Captain and three of his sailors were American born.
>
> The Custom House authorities think that the Captain and the crew of the *Celeste* conspired with the officers of the ship *Moorehead* [*sic*] to pick up the *Celeste* after they had abandoned her at sea, their purpose being to share the salvage. The drawback from the Custom House on the alcohol alone [i.e., the refund of excise on the value of the alcohol] amounts to $95,785. A reward for any knowledge of the crew was offered on Tuesday [25 March] by the Secretary of the Treasury, who states that the deck of the vessel was covered with blood stains. This is denied by the Custom House.

The newspaper misnamed the *Dei Gratia* as the *Moorehead*, presumably from her captain's name, which it got wrong like many others then and later. It's also baffling that it put a 'drawback' value of excise refund amounting to almost $100,000 on a cargo that Capt. Winchester in the *New York Herald* of 15 March 1873 noted was worth just $37,000.

And the Secretary of the Treasury, William Richardson, did not, in fact, offer a penny of 'reward' in his 25 March circular for information about the *Mary Celeste*.

News about the *Mary Celeste*, fake or otherwise, dried up soon after the end of the Gibraltar hearings. There was no news because, like Macavity, it wasn't there! *Mary Celeste* returned to her usual trade of transporting cargoes thither and yon. The early hopes were that the derelict's ten castaways might have been picked up by a passing ship and landed at a far-flung destination, then and there to re-emerge safe and sound. That optimism gradually faded, wrinkled, withered and died on the vine. Likewise Mr Solly-Flood's conviction that the disreputable miscreants of the crew would eventually somewhere crawl out from under a hiding-rock never materialised.

Ten years later a Canadian newspaper reminisced about the mysterious abandonment of the *Mary Celeste*. By then she had gone through various changes of ownership and crew. Virtually everything it reported about her discovery was bunkum – an 'old yarn', as it unwittingly perhaps admitted – from being encountered in the Mediterranean, to the orderly condition in which she was found, 'all sail set', and that her 'boats' were all 'in their places':

> Sudden Disappearance of a Ship's Captain and Crew – An Old Yarn Revived
> New York, May 29 [1883].– The American brig *Mary Celeste*, 268 tons register, under the command of Captain Bob Fleming, sailed from this port last week. Ten years ago a British merchantman sailing the Mediterranean saw the *Mary Celeste* a few miles to the leeward [*sic* – she was to windward of the *Dei Gratia*] with all sail set, yet behaving in such a manner that a sailor could see that something was wrong. Receiving no answer to their hail, they boarded her, and the sight that greeted them excited a feeling of intense curiosity.

That there was no one on board 'living or dead' was one of the few solid *facts* that followed:

> Every sail was set; the tiller was lashed fast; not a rope was out of place; everything below and aloft was in perfect order; a fire was burning quietly in the galley; dinner was standing untasted, and scarcely cold; the cargo in the hold was intact; the pumps were dry; no one, living or dead, was on board.
>
> The sailors searched vainly for an explanation of the sudden disappearance of the captain, his wife, his child, and crew. The log, written up to the hour of her discovery, showed that she hailed from

> Boston. There was not a drop of blood, lock of hair, disordered room, or anything to show signs of a struggle. The boats were in their places.
>
> There was not the slightest clue by which a reasonable hypothesis could be advanced to explain where the crew had gone, and from that day to this not the slightest clue has been obtained by owners, nor have they been able to frame an explanation of how she was abandoned, or hazard a guess as to why she was abandoned.
>
> Captain Fleming says that she has been a lucky ship ever since, that never a ghost or spook of those who vanished has ever appeared on her since.
>
> In the cabin a child's toys were scattered around and a piece of a woman's dress was still under the needle of the sewing machine.[12]

The article itself was not *fake* in the sense of deliberately falsified. Nor was it *news*, ten years on. It was just, in most of its elements, *wrong*. With the passage of time, bits of the *Mary Celeste* story, without the evidence to hand of the Gibraltar hearings, would branch into multi-shaped, multi-coloured offspring that bore some resemblance to a kernel of truth, but were misshapen and distorted and mangled by third- or fourth- or whatever-hand hybridising.

Errors of fact simply became repeated, perpetuated and metastasised. These were conflated into stories or reminiscences that derived from and resembled the known facts of the affair, but evolved along the lines of historical fiction.

'J. Habakuk Jephson's Statement', Anonymous (Arthur Conan Doyle)

The first of the *Mary Celeste* historical fictions was a short story published anonymously in the January 1884 edition of the British monthly literary journal, the *Cornhill Magazine*. The anonymous author of the story titled 'J. Habakuk Jephson's Statement' was later revealed to be Sir Arthur Conan Doyle (1859–1930), creator of the Sherlock Holmes sleuth, who first appeared in his novel *A Study in Scarlet* in 1887, four years after his *Cornhill* short story.

The name of the protagonist, Dr Habakuk Jephson, resonated from a minor Old Testament prophet, Habakkuk, who 'lived at the time when Judah was invaded by the Chaldeans, and taught that they were the instruments of God to punish the Jews for their lawlessness'. Dr Jephson's nemesis in his 'Statement' was the mixed-ethnicity Septimus Goring. He, not the victimised doctor, was actually the self-styled avenger of the 'lawlessness' that had persecuted black people and infected his conscience.

The story, it has to be said, was infused with racial, indeed racist caricatures that were familiar at the time, even as the protagonist claimed to be an ardent abolitionist in an era, and place, the United States, when slavery was being quashed, though not entirely extinguished. It revealed as much about ingrained traits of racism as it did about liberal attitudes to racial ideologies.

'J. Habakuk Jephson's Statement' was the first of a number of stories purported to have come from supposed survivors of the *Mary Celeste* abandonment. It began:

THE

CORNHILL MAGAZINE.

JANUARY, 1884.

J. HABAKUK JEPHSON'S STATEMENT.

IN the month of December in the year 1873 the British ship 'Dei Gratia' steered into Gibraltar, having in tow the derelict brigantine, 'Marie Celeste,' which had been picked up in latitude 38° 40′, longitude 17° 15′ West. There were several circumstances in connection with the condition and appearance of this abandoned vessel which excited considerable comment at the time, and aroused a curiosity which has never been satisfied. What these circumstances were was summed up in an able article which appeared in the 'Gibraltar Gazette.' The curious can find it in the issue for January 4, 1874, unless my memory deceives me. For the benefit of those, however, who may be unable to refer to the paper in question, I shall subjoin a few extracts which touch upon the leading features of the case.

VOL. II.— NO. 7, N. S. 1

First page of 'J. Habakuk Jephson's Statement'. (*Cornhill Magazine*, January 1884)

> In the month of December in the year 1873, the British ship *Dei Gratia* steered into Gibraltar, having in tow the derelict brigantine *Marie Celeste*, which it had picked up in latitude 38° 40', longitude 17° 15' West. There were several circumstances in connection with the condition and appearance of this abandoned vessel which excited considerable comment at the time, and aroused a curiosity which has never been satisfied.

The 'several circumstances', the story noted, were 'summed up in an article which appeared in the *Gibraltar Gazette*', the author's version of the *Gibraltar Chronicle*, 'in the issue for January 4, 1874, unless my memory deceives me'. His memory did deceive him, in that it was 1873. But no matter; the story continued with other misremembered details that characterised the fictitious nature of the narrative which occupied the first thirty-two pages of the magazine.

The author allowed that, as not everyone would be able 'to refer to the paper in question', he was disposed to 'subjoin a few extracts which touch upon the leading features of the case'. The 'extracts' certainly had a sense of authenticity. Many details, however, enmeshed in that milieu of authenticity, were decidedly dicey:

> The official log, which was found in the cabin, states that the vessel sailed from Boston to Lisbon, starting upon October 16. It is, however, most imperfectly kept, and affords little information. There is no reference to rough weather, and, indeed, the state of the vessel's paint and rigging excludes the idea that she was abandoned for any such reason.
>
> She is perfectly water-tight. No signs of a struggle or of violence are to be detected, and there is absolutely nothing to account for the disappearance of the crew.
>
> There are several indications that a lady was present on board, a sewing-machine being found in the cabin and some articles of female attire. These probably belonged to the captain's wife, who is mentioned in the log as having accompanied her husband. As an instance of the mildness of the weather, it may be remarked that a bobbin of

silk was found standing upon the sewing-machine, though the least roll of the vessel would have precipitated it to the floor.

The boats were intact, and slung upon the davits, and the cargo, consisting of tallow and American clocks, was untouched.

An old-fashioned sword of curious workmanship was discovered among some lumber in the forecastle, and this weapon is said to exhibit a longitudinal striation on the steel, as if it had recently been wiped. It has been placed in the hands of the police, and submitted to Dr. Monaghan, the analyst, for inspection …

We may remark, in conclusion, that Captain Dalton, of the *Dei Gratia*, an able and intelligent seaman, is of opinion that the *Marie Celeste* may have been abandoned a considerable distance from the spot at which she was picked up, since a powerful current runs up in that latitude from the African coast …

In the utter absence of a clue or grain of evidence, it is to be feared that the fate of the crew of the *Marie Celeste* will be added to those numerous mysteries of the deep which will never be solved until the great day when the sea shall give up its dead. If crime has been committed, as is much to be expected, there is little hope of bringing the perpetrators to justice.

More evidence of an imaginatively creative rather than a forensically attuned mind controlling the pen of the author came from his citation of details from 'a telegram from Boston' that 'represented the total amount of information which had been collected about the *Marie Celeste*', namely: that the vessel was 'of 170 tons burden'; that she 'belonged to White, Russell, & White, wine importers, of this city'; that the vessel's master was 'Captain J. W. Tibbs'; that he 'was accompanied by his wife, aged thirty-one, and their youngest child, five years old ["Doddy"]'; that 'the crew consisted of seven hands, including two coloured seamen, and a boy'; and that 'there were three passengers, one of whom was the well-known Brooklyn specialist on consumption [tuberculosis], Dr. Habakuk Jephson, who was a distinguished advocate for Abolition in the early days of the movement'.

The two other fictitious passengers were: 'Mr. J. Harton, a writer in the employ of the firm, and Mr. Septimus Goring, a half-caste gentleman, from New Orleans.'

Apart from a brief reference by the London shipping newspaper *Lloyd's List*, on 1 March 1873, this was the first time the *Mary Celeste* was rebranded as the *Marie Celeste*. It has been assumed pretty universally that Conan Doyle's story was the origin of that misnomer adopted over the years by many other mis-chroniclers of The Greatest Sea Mystery.

The protagonist of the short story was Joseph Habakuk Jephson, 'Doctor of Medicine of the University of Harvard, and ex-Consulting Physician of the Samaritan Hospital of Brooklyn'. His mission, he told readers, was to write 'all that I know of the ill-fated voyage ... before many months my tongue and hand may be alike incapable of conveying information'. In other words, before he was incapacitated very soon by some health condition to do so. The reason he had not 'proclaimed' the events of the *Mary/Marie Celeste* incident before, at least in writing, was, he said, that they were so categorically disbelieved and derided by those he had told the story to in the past.

The story went as follows.

In the years just before the American Civil War of the early 1860s and the abolition of slavery in the United States in 1865, Dr Jephson was vehemently opposed to slavery, a position he inherited from his father, a preacher and stout abolitionist. Jephson was wounded in the Civil War and taken to a home on a plantation to convalesce. There he was nursed back to health by, amongst other black servants, an aged woman named Martha.

One day Martha gave Jephson a kind of amulet, 'a flattish black stone with a hole through the middle', which she told him she could not take with her 'across the Jordan'. Her final admonition to Jephson – 'Keep it safe – nebber lose it!' – would guarantee, she said, that the stone would for ever protect him from any harm.

After the war, Jephson returned to Brooklyn to continue his medical practice. Some years later, his pulmonary health deteriorated.

A colleague recommended him 'to take a long sea-voyage'. A certain Mr Russell, whose firm, White, Russell & White, owned the '*Marie Celeste*', offered him passage in the ship which was about to leave from Boston on a voyage to Lisbon. Tibbs, her captain, Russell assured Jephson, 'is an excellent fellow', adding, 'There is nothing like a sailing ship for an invalid.'

Jephson 'arrived in Boston on October 12, 1873', to embark on what was destined to be a very strange, melodramatic and, indeed, ill-fated voyage. At the shipping firm's office he met one of the other passengers, a macabre and mysterious 'very tall, gaunt man' with 'a strong dash of negro blood in him'. His name was Mr Septimus Goring, who impressed Jephson in more ways than one:

> His complexion was of a sickly, unhealthy yellow, and as his face was deeply pitted with smallpox, the general impression was so unfavourable as to be almost revolting. When he spoke, however, it was in a soft, melodious voice, and in well-chosen words, and he was evidently a man of some education.

As Goring was about to sign on for the voyage, Jephson 'was horrified to observe that the fingers of his right hand had been lopped off', such that he could not 'recall any sight which gave me such a thrill of disgust as that great brown sponge-like hand with the single member protruding from it'. The other passenger, John Harton, an accountant, was travelling to Lisbon 'in the interests of [his] firm'.

From 16 October, when the voyage began, Jephson kept a journal 'in order to vary the monotony of the long sea-voyage'. One of his first jottings was that Capt. Tibbs was less than happy about having to replace two sailors who failed to show up, with 'a couple of negroes who happened to be on the quay', and who, Jephson opined, 'may take a spell at the wheel or swab the decks', but would be 'of little or no use in rough weather'.

Septimus Goring himself was accompanied by his own young black servant, such that Jephson noted 'we are rather a piebald community'.

From the start, then, there were intimations of racial tensions on the '*Marie Celeste*'.

The accountant John Harton, though, was 'a cheery, amusing young fellow':

> Strange how little wealth has to do with happiness! He [Harton] has all the world before him and is seeking his fortune in a far land, yet he is as transparently happy as a man can be. Goring is rich, if I am not mistaken, and so am I; but I know that I have a lung, and Goring has some deeper trouble still, to judge by his features. How poorly do we both contrast with the careless, penniless clerk!

The mysterious and deformed Septimus Goring, though apparently learned and wealthy, was of interest to Jephson 'as a psychological study'. Goring added a gothic melancholy to the narrative. On one drizzly, cold day that confined Jephson to his cabin when he was feeling 'weak and depressed':

> Goring came in to see me, but his company did not tend to cheer me up much, as he hardly uttered a word, but contented himself with staring at me in a peculiar and rather irritating manner. He then got up and stole out of the cabin without saying anything. I am beginning to suspect that the man is a lunatic.

A few days later:

> A misfortune has occurred so unexpected and so horrible that my little escape of the morning [Goring's accidental shooting of a pistol in the cabin next to Jephson's] dwindles into insignificance. Mrs. Tibbs and her child have disappeared – utterly and entirely disappeared.

Jephson assumed that Mrs Tibbs and little Doddy had fallen overboard during the night and drowned, though he mused: 'The whole affair is wrapped in mystery ... Whatever the truth may be it is a terrible catastrophe, and has cast the darkest gloom upon our voyage.' An even darker gloom settled upon Capt. Tibbs. A few days later:

> *October 24.*– Is the ship accursed? Was there ever a voyage which began so fairly and which changed so disastrously? Tibbs shot himself through the head during the night.

After his body was consigned to the deep, Jephson reflected:

> The sooner we reach Lisbon and get away from this accursed ship the better pleased shall I be. I feel as though we were in a floating coffin.

A scrapbook of newspaper cuttings about unsolved murders over twenty years that belonged to Goring, which accountant Harton found on deck, deepened the mysterious character of Goring. Still, the voyage quietened down, as Jephson noted in his journal, with a domestic detail of the real *Mary Celeste* voyage:

> Were it not for Mrs. Tibbs' sewing-machine upon a side-table we might forget the unfortunate family had ever existed.

One morning on deck, Jephson was showing his stone amulet to Harton. Goring appeared and asked if he might show the stone to the helmsman, one of the black sailors, to see what he thought of it. The helmsman appeared to be astonished by it and countenanced it 'with some reverence'. Goring told Jephson that the helmsman had thought it worthless, so Goring tried to throw it overboard. The black helmsman stayed his hand and returned the amulet to Jephson 'with a low bow and every sign of profound respect':

> When I compare the effect produced by the stone upon the sailor ... with the respect shown to Martha on the plantation, and the surprise of Goring on its first production, I cannot but come to the conclusion that I have really got hold of some powerful talisman

> which appeals to the whole dark race. I must not trust it in Goring's hands again.

Jephson ended his journal on the day, 'November 13', that 'a most extraordinary event … happened, so extraordinary as to be almost inexplicable'. The ship, to everyone's surprise, had reached a coast that was determined to be 'the mainland of Africa', with 'a great sandy waste' visible past the 'long line of surf, great, green billows' breaking on the shore. The stand-in captain, Hyson, declared that 'the instruments had been tampered with', which had put the vessel so far off her course towards Portugal.

That night Jephson was summoned by Goring's 'little black page' to go up on deck. There he was assailed, gagged and bound by the black crew under Septimus Goring's command. A dark body lay crouched at his feet in the darkness:

> Glancing down, I saw that the man who had been crouching on the deck was still lying there, and as I gazed at him, a flickering ray of moonlight fell full upon his upturned face. Great Heaven! Even now, when more than twelve years have elapsed, my hand trembles as I write that, in spite of distorted features and projecting eyes, I recognised the face of Harton, the cheery young clerk who had been my companion during the voyage. It needed no medical eye to see that he was quite dead, while the twisted handkerchief round the neck, and the gag in his mouth, showed the silent way in which the hell-hounds had done their work.
>
> The clue which explained every event of our voyage came upon me like a flash of light as I gazed on poor Harton's corpse. Much was dark and unexplained, but I felt a great dim perception of the truth.

Goring and 'the four ruffians' under his direction, all armed with knives, Goring with a pistol, stood by the rail. A canoe full of men, 'a swarm of gigantic negroes', had come off from the shore and clambered onto the ship. An elder amongst the group took the black stone amulet from Jephson's pocket and scrutinised it. Goring spoke to Jephson:

> 'You will bear me witness,' he said in his softest accents, 'that I am no party to sparing your life. If it rested with me you would die as these other men are about to do. I have no personal grudge against either you or them, but I have devoted my life to the destruction of the white race, and you are the first that has ever been in my power and has escaped me.
>
> 'You may thank that stone of yours for your life. These poor fellows reverence it, and indeed if it really be what they think it is they have cause. Should it prove when we get ashore that they are mistaken, and that its shape and material is a mere chance, nothing can save your life ...'

The assailants bundled Jephson into a canoe. A few moments later, 'a hundred yards or so from the ship', he heard 'a sort of dull, moaning sound, followed by a succession of splashes in the water'. The ship, now deserted, 'was left drifting about – a dreary, spectre-like hulk. Nothing was taken from her by the savages. The whole fiendish transaction was carried through as decorously and temperately as though it were a religious rite.'

On shore Jephson was taken to a village, in the centre of which was an imposing building which turned out to be a kind of temple. Inside was a statue 'admirably cut in jet-black stone'. An elder of the village, holding Jephson's amulet-talisman and 'stretching up his arm fitted Martha's black stone on to a jagged surface on the statue's head' from which the stone had clearly broken off:

> The group round me prostrated themselves upon the ground at the sight with a cry of reverence, while the crowd outside, to whom the result was communicated, set up a wild whooping and cheering.

That night Goring went into a hut where Jephson was lying on 'a couch of skins'. He explained that, as he supposed, he was 'returning good for evil, for I have come to help you to escape'. He wanted, he said, 'to be king over these fellows', but Jephson's deity status had 'turned all their heads, so that they think you are come down from heaven, and my influence will be gone until you are out of the way'.

He explained how the villagers, as 'Mahometans', originated from a schism among the followers of 'Mahomet' who took away from Arabia into Africa 'a valuable relic of their old faith in the shape of a large piece of the black stone of Mecca'. This was carved as the statue then placed in the temple at the centre of the village. An ear broken from it, Jephson's amulet, was taken away by some of the tribe who, years later, wandered away to the south. A tradition arose amongst the villagers that the ear would one day return, as Goring told Jephson, 'and you have had the honour of fulfilling the prophecy.'

But the other, greater reason Goring wanted to help Jephson escape was that he wanted him to take a message back 'to the white race, the great dominating race whom I hate and defy'. He had, he said, 'warred against the whole white race as they for centuries had warred against the black one'.

To avenge the grotesque injury of his mutilated hand, inflicted upon him 'by a white man's knife', and his mother, a slave, lashed to death, and his wife killed, too, he had murdered whites 'from Maine to Florida, and from Boston to San Francisco ... deaths which baffled the police' for twenty years. Hence the scrapbook of newspaper cuttings of unsolved murders that Harton found lying on the deck of the '*Marie Celeste*'.

Tiring of the blood he had shed, Goring 'determined to find some bold free black people and to throw in my lot with them, to cultivate their latent powers, and to form a nucleus for a great coloured nation'. That was how he came to be a voyager on the '*Marie Celeste*', and why it was he who had manipulated her compasses and chronometer to deviate her course according to his own navigation and instructions to the black helmsmen. And why it was he, Septimus Goring, who had pushed Mrs Tibbs and her daughter overboard and shot Capt. Tibbs:

> I had bargained that all on board should die; but that stone of yours upset my plans. I also bargained that there should be no plunder.

> No one can say we are pirates. We have acted from principle, not from any sordid motive.

And so Septimus Goring set Dr J. Habakuk Jephson into a small boat which the two black sailors from the '*Marie Celeste*' helped get through the surf to the open sea, before swimming back ashore. On the fifth day he was picked up by a passing steamer and landed at Liverpool, from where he returned home to New York. After many years, he 'put the facts before the public as they occurred, careless how far they may be believed', as 'J. Habakuk Jephson's Statement'. It ended:

> Turn to your map of Africa. There above Cape Blanco ... it is that Septimus Goring still reigns over his dark subjects, unless retribution has overtaken him; and there ... Harton lies with Hyson and the other poor fellows who were done to death in the *Marie Celeste*.

Conan Doyle's short story is a literary gem. It has overtones of Joseph Conrad's sea novel set on the trading ship *Narcissus*. It speaks of great themes: of the relationships between good and evil, power and humanity and compassion, and the morality of retribution and salvation.

Mr Solly-Flood's Reaction

Frederick Solly-Flood had stepped down as Gibraltar's Attorney General in 1877 'on account of increasing years and infirmities', according to one of his obituaries. He took umbrage at the Conan Doyle story, having first, apparently, taken it at face value as a factual narrative of the *Mary Celeste* affair. He dashed off a letter to a Gibraltar journal, the *Mons Calpe* (the Roman name for the Rock of Gibraltar), exclaiming his indignation at the story's inaccuracies but most particularly its pernicious racial implications.

> An instance of the amusing results which sometimes proceed from an entire absence of the sense of humour is afforded by a letter published lately in a Gibraltar journal, the Mons Calpe, from a Mr. Solly Flood, late 'Her Majesty's Advocate-General.' In the January number of the *Cornhill Magazine* appeared a powerful and somewhat ghastly story, entitled 'J. Habakkuk Jephson's Statement,' which purported to be an account of the diabolical murder of the captain of the brigantine Marie Celeste, his wife, child, and the crew, by a half-caste American. The story was altogether sensational and improbable; ...
>
> What does the matter-of-fact Mr. Solly Flood do? In all good faith he writes a long letter, in which, after disproving officially and in detail many incidents of the narrative, he solemnly declares that 'the statement is, in point of fact, a fabrication from beginning to end,' and dwells on the wickedness of imputing crimes to the citizens of the United States, 'especially the coloured population.'[13]

Frederick Solly-Flood was something of an eccentric. He might well have been regarded as a pompous diva. An obituary described him as 'an old public servant' with an 'incisive personality'. He played his central role in The Greatest Sea Mystery with conviction. His rebuke of racism in the 'fabrication' that was 'J. Habakuk Jephson's Statement' was, however, a kind of moral recalibration to rebalance the weight of whatever other blemishes might have weighed against his character.

The *Mary Celeste* case did not define Mr Solly-Flood's life. It was never mentioned in his obituaries, though that was because it had not yet evolved from an ordinary mystery of the sea to become The Greatest Sea Mystery. But in certain ways Mr Solly-Flood defined some aspects of the mystery – the assertions of violence, of an escaped mob of murderers, of homicidal conspiracy – that have ensured his prominent role in the drama of its mythology.

Mr Solly-Flood died in Gibraltar on 13 May 1888 at the age of 86. An obituary of him read, in part:

> He was a man of great wit, vivacity, and eloquence, and he preserved his physical vigour and love of athletic exercise until almost the last ... Mr. Solly Flood lived and died in a lonely house high up on the rock, embedded in orange and lemon trees, and looking out over the Atlantic, where he usually gave 'an English leg of mutton dinner party' once a week to the society of the place after the P. and O. steamer had brought out the homely but much coveted delicacy in a refrigerator.

Misinformation

In December 1885, the year the *Mary Celeste* was sunk on a Haitian reef, several articles appeared in American newspapers about her unsolved mystery of 1872. Their compilation of errors revealed as much about the corrosiveness of truth by the passage of time – and not much time, at that – as about the factual reality of the *Mary Celeste* mystery. An interview with an American consular official who related 'interesting stories about consuls and their work' included the *Mary Celeste* incident. Most of the details were, indeed, 'interesting', but mainly in how far they diverged from truth:

> There is one mystery that the consuls have not been so successful in as the cases I have just related. In February, 1876, the *Marie Celeste*, an American merchant vessel, put out from New York for Villefranche. She had on board thirteen persons, including the captain's wife and little daughter. Some time afterwards she was sighted off Gibraltar by a French steamer. The Frenchmen gazed long and earnestly at the vessel, standing almost still under full sail. Glasses failed to discover any signs of life on board of her.
>
> The steamer bore down upon the *Marie Celeste* and the captain hailed her, but received no response. A boat was then sent to her and the crew boarded her. What a surprise was in store for them. Everything was in apple-pie order, but there was not a soul on board.

> The vessel was searched from stem to stern. There were no signs of a struggle. The boats were all there; clothes were hanging out to dry.
>
> In the cabin was a half-finished meal on the table; a piece of sewing was on the machine in the cabin; the compasses and watches of the captain and mate were found; there was plenty of water on board, and altogether it was a most unaccountable mystery what had become of the thirteen people.
>
> Of course the number was thirteen, and this may account for their disappearance.
>
> The ship's log had been kept until within forty-two hours of the time when she was discovered, and only spoke of a prosperous voyage, and without accident of any kind. An examination of the unfinished meal proved the viands to be pure. It was with difficulty a crew was secured to take the vessel to its destination.
>
> Since [then] she has run between New York and the West Indies. About two years ago she was sunk by her captain to secure the insurance, but he got a long term in the penitentiary for his pains [*sic* – Capt. Parker was not convicted in the trial, much less jailed; he died three months after the trial].
>
> The consuls throughout the world were informed of the circumstances, and were instructed to solve the mystery, but though nine years have elapsed, nothing has been heard of the crew of the *Marie Celeste*.[14]

Sailors then were a particularly suspicious breed. The number thirteen presaged ill-fortune. It became common in *Mary Celeste* chronicles to number the souls on board at that ominous total. And so, naturally, 'this may account for their disappearance'.

Another newspaper article appeared around the same time in the *Washington Post*, reprinted in the *Daily Alta California* on 16 December 1885, that perpetrated almost as much misinformation, and with similarly confounding inaccuracies. The 'Deep and Unsolved Ocean Mystery' of the '*Marie Celeste*' was, it said, 'the weirdest and most unaccountable story in the annals of history or fiction'.

The history of the story wasn't entirely fiction, though a good many of the reported details were.

The incident, it said, happened 'nine years ago'; it was, in fact, thirteen years before. The misnamed '*Marie Celeste*' was by then a common error, as was the 'thirteen souls on board'. Her destination of 'Villefranche', or 'Villa Franche', might have surfaced and bobbed about here (and elsewhere) from a reference to the port that Capt. Shufeldt's ship, the USS *Plymouth*, had come from, before stopping at Gibraltar long enough for Consul Sprague to get him to examine the *Mary Celeste*.

The vessel that came across the '*Marie Celeste*' was said to be 'an outward-bound British bark', which it was – outward-bound, that is; not a bark (barque). The men from her who went in a boat to board the derelict included, fictitiously, the 'Captain, with a crew of picked men'. There they found that 'the boats were all suspended from their davits'. The by now ubiquitous fiction of 'a half-eaten meal was found', this time 'upon the seamen's table', as was, on a table in the master's cabin, 'the remains of an interrupted dinner'. A mysteriously oft-repeated 'fact' was that the last entry in the *Mary Celeste*'s log book 'was dated forty-two hours before the arrival of the Britisher', meaning the *Dei Gratia*. Why forty-two hours?

An addendum to the story was that the US State Department had received 'numbers of communications purporting to be explanations of the case':

> The most probable perhaps of all was one received from a Frenchman, who suggested that the cook for some reason or other had become enraged against the captain and all the crew, and had put poison in the meal, which had been found uneaten. In this way he had killed everybody, and had then thrown their bodies overboard. Overpowered by the enormity of his crime, he then committed suicide by throwing himself into the sea.

The article countered that proposition with reasons that undermined it but averred nevertheless that: 'No suggestion has ever come nearer the truth than this, however, and the case still remains an unexplained mystery of the sea.' This implied that the writer of the article actually *knew* the truth of the matter – which, of course, no one did; which is why it was 'an unexplained mystery of the sea' – including the mystery of how such fictions of fact came to infect and inflect the documented, evidentiary truth of the *Mary Celeste* incident, from the Gibraltar hearings, over so many years.

To be fair, hardly anyone even knew the evidence was documented and lying dormant in some government archive in Gibraltar. By and large, the 'facts' were cribbed from other newspaper reports, or half-remembered by newsroom cronies, or cobbled together at whatever factual cost to meet an editor's deadline for a few hundred words by press-time. Or combinations of the above, with a dash, and often more like a hearty helping of fantasy fiction.

Jacob Hammell's Story

'Dr J. Habakuk Jephson' was the first and probably most fabulously fictitious survivor of the *Mary Celeste* to write a declaration of what supposedly explained the mystery of the deserted vessel and how he survived. In 1897 another ostensible remnant of the '*Marie Celeste*' incident, a certain 'Jacob Hammell', turned up in the Peruvian seaport of Iquique to tell the tall tale of his survival before he shuffled off this mortal coil. The sceptical headline of the story in the *Portland Daily Press* of Portland, Maine, on 6 November 1897, was spun out rather melodramatically as:

> A Tale of the Sea – The Disappearance of the Crew of the *Marie Celeste* – A Dying Sailor's Story of an Ocean Mystery – It Recalls a Famous Case and Introduces Into Its History Three Murders – It Reads Like the Delusion of a Wandering Mind and That Is Very Likely What it Is

The story itself then began:

> By the confession of a dying man, the greatest of all the great mysteries of the sea has been explained away; a mystery which for years baffled the intelligence, the ingenuity and the imagination of people in every walk of life the world over. On his death-bed, in far-off Iquique, Peru, one Jacob Hammell has given to the world the strange abandonment of the famous American brig *Marie Celeste*, the story of which has long since passed into the list of unfathomable puzzles of the ocean.

It followed with a summary of the *Mary Celeste* incident which included the usual culprits of preposterous particulars and some novelties besides, namely:

'... a British ship, homeward bound from the East Indies, sighted a vessel, under all plain sails, off the northwest coast of Africa';

'In the cabin, the captain's wife had evidently been sewing when the sudden departure [i.e., abandonment] was ordered, as her sewing machine was open, with some sewing still in it.'

'A candle-stick was still standing which, with other evidence, showed that the weather was smooth when the flight took place';

'... dinner was being cooked in the galley, the embers of the fire still being warm';

'... the mysterious craft was towed into Gibraltar by the rescuing ship.'

The investigations at Gibraltar, it claimed, revealed that 'some spots on the deck were found ... to be chicken blood, as might have been expected, as a fowl was being prepared for the captain's dinner when the vessel was discovered'. Most alarming, and wholly untrue, with the obvious confusion of the name of the *Mary Celeste*'s mate with that of her captain, was the claim that:

> ... in the investigations by the State Department in Washington, it was found that the mate of the *Marie Celeste*, a man named Briggs, had, just before his last voyage, sold out his home and belongings in Brooklyn, N.Y., and his family had gone, no one knows whither to this day. No trace of them could ever be found. The property sold for a goodly sum, and it is thought that Briggs had other property; he certainly had money in a savings bank, which he also drew out before this voyage.

'Such', the article continued, 'was the state of affairs on July 21 last [1897], when a man, in the last stages of consumption, in a sailors' boarding house in Iquique, summoned a fellow boarder, and, telling him he was about to die, and would not, in all probability, live another day, asked him to listen to a story which he had on his mind, a story which he thought the world ought to know.'

The 'fellow boarder' was apparently 'a man of rather more intelligence than the average boarder at such places'. The listener later arrived in San Francisco and declared that 'the substance of [Hammell's] confession' was as follows, 'the man having died two days later':

> My name is Jacob Hammell. I was the second mate of the ship which fell in with the brig *Marie Celeste*, and was the first one to board her, going alongside in the yawl, which was pulled by two seamen. I left them in the boat when I went on board. Those men, if they can be found, will tell you that I was on board over half an hour before I again communicated with them.
>
> When I got on board the *Celeste*, the first person I saw was the cook. He told me that he, the captain and the captain's wife, were the only living people on board, small-pox having carried off all the others within the past two weeks. I went into the cabin, where I found the captain's wife at the sewing machine. The captain was in his bunk, very bad off with small-pox, too weak to do much more than lie very low.
>
> They seemed sorry at having me come on board, and the captain finally told me that he had small-pox on board, but that he did not want it known, as it would quarantine him when he reached port and also make it hard to dispose of his cargo. For this reason he had taken care to make no mention in the log of the disease nor of the deaths or burials of those who had died.
>
> Then his wife told me that the mate had died the day before, and asked me if I wouldn't help the cook bury him. Then she let slip the fact that the mate had a large sum of money in his room, which he was taking to go to South Africa with, where he was going to be joined by his family and start in some kind of business.

> I did as she asked me, but as I was sewing up the mate's body an idea entered my head. I followed it up, and to this idea of mine is due the mystery of the *Marie Celeste*. I carried out my scheme to the letter. When the mate's body was all ready, the cook and I took it to the weather gangway; he wanted to take it, as usual, to the lee side, but I objected. As we lurched it over I gave a twist to the line attached to the body, threw it over the cook, and in a second he was overboard, going down like a shot with the weighted corpse.
>
> Then I got the captain's wife on deck, and arranged to have her stand on the weather gangway for a moment – just long enough for me to throw a tarpaulin over her and heave her overboard. I found it easy enough with the captain, he was so feeble. I just lifted him out of his bunk, and he didn't suspect what was up until I had him half through the cabin port.
>
> Then I went out and told the men in the boat that the brigantine was abandoned, that I had looked all over her, alow and aloft, and could find nobody. One of them came aboard, at my order, and saw for himself. I then sent them back to our ship with a message for the captain.
>
> While they were gone I rummaged in the mate's cabin and soon found a tin box, which I opened with a marlinespike. In it I found over 1,600 pounds, every bit in Bank of England notes. There was also a little English gold. These, with a five-pound note I had of my own, I left in his chest.
>
> That's all the story you need to know, except that I let go one boat, with the plug out, while the men were away.

The seaman who recounted Hammell's tall tale was, the article continued, one Carl Johanson, 'a mariner by trade' who had 'sailed on several American coasters' but 'deserted several years ago in South America, in Valparaiso, Chili, he says'.

The best that can be said of Hammell's confession is a comment on it in another newspaper piece about the *Mary Celeste* from 1911, titled 'Tragedy Of Old Ocean: Disappearance of Captain and Crew Never Was Satisfactorily Explained':

> This absurd story was first published in San Francisco and later found its way to Maine. It was, on the face of it, a pure invention, like the story of the murder of the captain.

The 'murder of the captain' referred to an earlier story, in 1877:

> ... to the effect that Mate Richardson had been seen hiding in the West Indies, and that he and members of the crew had murdered the captain and stolen many thousands of dollars that the vessel was carrying. As a matter of fact, the *Mary Celeste* carried no money of any amount.

And, as another matter of fact, Jacob Hammell's story wasn't even a particularly good one: what happened, for instance, to the money and the 'little English gold' he found? That denouement – 'That's all the story you need to know' – was left dangling in the breeze like an Irish pennant.

Still, as salty yarns go, the confession of triple homicide on the high seas by a dying man was probably enough to be getting on with.

Arthur Cocker's Claim

In May 1937, a man named Arthur Cocker, reported to be the captain of a barge, *Humber Lady*, from Hull, on the north-east coast of England, piped up that he was 'the only man living who [had] any first-hand connection with the mystery' of the *Mary Celeste*. His connection, he said, was that he sailed on a ship that came across the abandoned vessel, 'and was actually the second boat to come upon the mystery ship', chirped the *Hull Daily Mail* on 17 May 1937:

> The skipper, Mr. Arthur Cocker, told a reporter that he was a cabin boy on one of the grain traders which came upon the *Marie Celeste*. It was the Kentishman, and was actually the second boat to come upon the mystery.

> 'All the sails were set and the deck in complete order,' he said. 'The only sign of foul play was a blood-stained hatchet buried deep in the mainmast. In certain shipping circles [Lloyd's, apparently, which actually had nothing to do with insurance on the *Mary Celeste*] I have made application for salvage money,' Mr. Cocker added, 'but it has been refused.
>
> 'I have, however, documents and notebooks taken from the captain's cabin of the *Marie Celeste* which have never been seen. The revelations they contain will, in my opinion, throw an entirely new light on the mystery.'

Another report added: 'Capt. Cocker's theory is that someone aboard went berserk, and killed two or three of the crew before being killed himself. Then the remainder of the crew became frightened and took to the boats when they saw other vessels on the horizon."[15]

Capt. Cocker's documents, 'taken from the captain's cabin of the *Marie Celeste*', had 'never been seen' because, of course, they did not exist. The only 'entirely new light' they threw on the mystery was the flash of lightning 'revelation' from the old barge skipper which, as suddenly, clapped out with a rumble of thunder, and that was the last ever heard about it. The 'blood-stained hatchet buried deep in the mainmast' was, however, a nice touch.

'The Case of the Marie Celeste: An Ocean Mystery' by J.L. Hornibrook

Chambers's Journal was, like the *Cornhill Magazine*, a popular British periodical that published a range of 'Tales and Stories', 'Articles of Instruction and Entertainment', and miscellaneous writings on 'Science and Arts' and poetry.

J.L. Hornibrook's rather brief account of the *Mary Celeste* mystery appeared in the 17 September 1904 edition of *Chambers's Journal*. Not much is known about the author. John Laurence Hornibrook seems to have been born in Croydon, Surrey, in 1864. He became a journalist and wrote a few novels (*The Shadow of a Life*, published in 1888, was the most popular), was awarded an MBE (Member of the Order of the British Empire) in the 1918 New Year's Honours and died in Suffolk in 1934.

His 1904 *Chambers's* article began with a novelistic rather than journalistic treatment of the *Mary Celeste* facts, though, by then, after the plethora of *Mary Celeste* fact-fictions, it was sometimes hard to distinguish between the two:

> On a certain morning, back in the sixties [i.e., 1860s], the Spanish authorities near the Straits of Gibraltar noticed a vessel in the offing which speedily attracted special attention. She was a brig, with all sails set, and at first sight appeared to be heading direct for the Straits, as though to enter the Mediterranean.

So far, so typically wrong in most respects. The vessel 'wobbled about and veered round with every changing puff of wind as if bereft of a guiding hand and left to stagger blindly onward of her own accord'. A truth! Within a few sentences, after the boat's boarding party reached 'the strange vessel', the novelistic gears of the author re-engaged:

> A minute examination of the vessel revealed a truly extraordinary and astounding state of affairs. There was not a single boat missing. They were all in their proper places, slung on the davits and stowed on deck in the usual manner. Further than that, not a rope or stay, not a sail or spar, was injured. Everything, from truck to keel, was as sound as the day the vessel had sailed ... and on the cabin was found the remains of a half-consumed dinner, apparently as fresh as when it came from the cook's galley.

Oh, the 'half-consumed dinner'! As regular a cliché in *Mary Celeste* narratives as the 'all sails set' image of a vessel 'under full sail'. Hornibrook, MBE, continued:

> The brig was navigated into Gibraltar, and there the American consul came on board, for, as was seen by the name of her port on the stern, she hailed from Boston. He, in turn, proceeded to make a minute and searching inspection, overhauling the vessel from stem to stern, and noting every detail. The only fresh discovery was something which looked like the slash of an axe or cutlass on the bulwark forward; but this, in itself, was calculated to throw little light on the mystery ...
>
> The *Marie Celeste* set sail from Boston under the most favourable circumstances, and certainly there was nothing in her complement or otherwise to warrant the assumption that the voyage would result in tragedy of any kind. She was an ordinary trading brig, bound for the Mediterranean ports with a general cargo of merchandise. Her crew consisted of seventeen hands[!], composed chiefly of Americans, Danes, and Norwegians. In addition there was the captain, his wife, and their little daughter – twenty souls, all told ...

> From that day to this the fate of these twenty souls has remained an inscrutable and insoluble mystery.

The author went on to dismiss 'the various theories advanced in explanation of this singular ocean mystery', including: piracy; desertion of a ship thought to be on the verge of foundering – 'for not a single boat was missing'; stormy weather that swept everybody overboard; an attack of madness that compelled them all to 'voluntarily cast themselves into the sea'; or a homicidal maniac amongst the crew who 'murdered his fellows' en masse.

Author Hornibrook finally got around to his personal preference about how the *Mary Celeste* was emptied of all its 'twenty souls' and left derelict – a truly Brobdingnagian whopper of a 'solution' to the mystery:

> One truly startling and surprising theory would seem to cover the entire facts. American scientists were consulted at the time as to the possibility of the catastrophe being due to the attack of some terrible monster of the deep. They scouted [rejected] the idea. We have now, however, a much more intimate and extensive knowledge of these sea-monsters; and the theory alluded to attributes the disappearance of the crew to the agency of a huge octopus or devil-fish [giant squid]. The scene might be depicted somewhat as follows:
>
> There is a man stationed at the wheel. He is alone on deck, all the others having gone below to their mid-day meal. Suddenly a huge octopus rises from the deep, and rearing one of its terrible arms aloft encircles the helmsman. His yells bring every soul on board rushing on deck. One by one they are caught by the waving, wriggling arms and swept overboard. Then, freighted with its living load, the monster slowly sinks into the deep again, leaving no traces of its attack.
>
> It may be pointed out, in support of this theory, that the mark of a slash on the bulwark of the vessel would look as if some member of the crew had seized an axe and attempted to chop off one of the threatening arms. If, however, the theory be not accepted, it must be left to the reader's imagination to furnish a better one.

Hornibrook's suggestion was that, if the reader couldn't believe that a gigantic kraken-like cephalopod had risen out of the deep, grabbed all seventeen sailors, the captain, his wife and child and dragged them into the abyss, 'leaving no traces of its attack' – well, have you got a better one?!

Accounts of large, vicious and violent octopus-type creatures, including, later, giant squid, as descriptions of curiosities of the deep, were in fashion throughout the nineteenth century (but in earlier centuries, too). Traces of Hornibrook's story came from an article written by a regular columnist on scientific matters in the *Illustrated London News*, Dr Andrew Wilson, titled 'The Mystery of the *Marie Celeste*', published on 16 September 1899. It started with familiar misinformation that Hornibrook later adopted:

> Did you ever hear the story of the *Marie Celeste*, a brig which sailed from Boston in the 'sixties, bound for Mediterranean ports with a general cargo of merchandise? No.
>
> Well, you shall hear it as I heard it told the other night by a friend over a pipe and something else which cheers the heart of man. I shall tell you the story as it was told to me, a plain unvarnished tale, the details of which are writ large in the records of the American Foreign Office, or whatever bureau in Washington corresponds to our own department at home that looks after the affairs of other folks [he meant the US State Department].
>
> This is no mere myth or fiction of the sea, but a sober tale of fact, and when I have told the story – I hope I shall relate it circumspectly – my readers will have presented to them as pretty a puzzle as ever was set before the mind of man to solve. So far as I know, it has never been solved yet.

This 'sober tale of fact' started with the fallacy that the '*Marie Celeste*' 'set sail from Boston with a crew of seventeen hands' and the captain and his wife and daughter, 'twenty souls all told'. It followed up with her being found in the Straits of Gibraltar 'within hail of the Spanish coast', that 'all her sails were set', and that 'the Spanish authorities hailed the brig, without receiving any answer to their signals'. She was boarded 'by the coastguard I presume' who, of course, discovered no one on board.

Inspections of the vessel revealed nothing untoward about her condition: 'Everything from truck to keel was in its proper place.' The obligatory 'half-eaten dinners' were mentioned. Dr Wilson was enthusiastic about one particular detail:

> The brig's boats – note this fact, please – were all on board slung on their davits or stowed on deck.

Dr Wilson noted that 'strict inquiries were made in both America and Europe concerning captain and crew'. Sailors' Homes were notified 'in case some derelict seaman should have come to a restful haven therein'. The nationalities of the crew 'included Americans, Danes, Norwegians, and men of other nations in their numbers'. And so on and so forth until he got round to possible reasons for the vessel's desertion:

> Pirates and a wholesale slaughter of the crew by ordinary murder or by walking the plank? Nonsense. Piracy was no more common in the Atlantic in the 'sixties than it is now ... The pirate idea clearly will not hold water at all.

Nor, he considered, would storm, illness or insanity 'leading to homicidal slaying of the others', as he said, 'hold water'. Dr Wilson was having no truck with such nonsense. Instead he offered up a notion, 'in all modesty', that was rejected by 'American scientists [who] were consulted regarding the possibilities of catastrophe arising from the denizens of the sea themselves':

> But we know more about certain sea monsters in this year of grace than they did in the 'sixties, and my explanation of the mystery of the *Marie Celeste* is that which attributes the disappearance of the crew to the attack of a huge octopus, or devil-fish, or of some other member of the cuttlefish group.

Let me picture what I think may have happened.

And so Dr Wilson envisaged 'a man at the wheel'. And the rest of the 'picture' was virtually as J.L. Hornibrook borrowed it five years later, after 'a huge octopus rises from the deep' to create the mayhem that cleared all 'twenty souls' off the '*Marie Celeste*'. He supported his rationale for the theory of calamary calamity by ending:

> If we find squids, which are cousins of the octopus, forty and fifty feet long, if octopi abound in Southern seas with bodies as big as vats and arms twenty feet in length – these things we know – we may go farther and far worse in our attempt to explain this mystery of the deep.

McClure's Magazine, May 1905

Just after Hornibrook's 1904 giant octopus 'solution', an article appeared in the American monthly magazine *McClure's*, in May 1905, titled 'The Terror of the Sea', about derelict ships. The author, P.T. McGrath, included the *Mary Celeste* affair amongst his overview of mysterious derelicts, 'a more fantastic creation, apparently, than novelist ever wove'. Almost everything he described about her was wrong: that 'she left New York in 1887'; that 'her personnel [numbered] thirteen'; that, when the boarding party from 'a British bark' investigated, 'everything was in its place – even the boats at the davits', and so on, including a novelty that 'an awning covered the poop' deck.

One of the few truths was McGrath's conclusion that 'from that day to this the mystery has never been unravelled'. He offered no theoretical solution himself. But his defective version of events was emblematic of how distorted the reality of the *Mary Celeste* mystery had become within a generation of her puzzling abandonment.

'Alternative facts' are both quick growers and virulent in their tenacity to infect the truth.

'Mystery of the Mary Celeste' by John Ball Osborne

Over the decades a parade of hack journalists, opportune editors and imaginative fictionists contributed numerous stories of mangled facts about the *Mary Celeste*. There sometimes emerged, however, a genuine, real McCoy who actually knew their stuff and wrote pieces of substance. Such was John Ball Osborne.

Born at Wilkes-Barre, Pennsylvania, in 1868, Osborne became an officer in the American Foreign Service, under the aegis of the then Department of State, as Consul General in a number of European postings in the early twentieth century. He graduated from Yale University in 1889. His appointment as US Consul at Ghent, Belgium, in the same year, by President Benjamin Harrison, at the age of 21, made him the youngest ever US consular appointee. Osborne's last Consul General post was at Budapest, after which he retired, in 1933, and died in Washington, DC, on 2 October 1954, aged 86.

In 1906 Osborne wrote one of the most considered and correct accounts of the *Mary Celeste* mystery from the early years. The piece was published in the *Evening Star* newspaper of Washington, DC, and the *New York Tribune*, both on 20 May 1906. It was unusual, for the time, because of its attention to factual detail about the truth, as far as was then known, of the *Mary Celeste* mystery. What was interesting, considering his consular career, was how he came to the case.

> While looking through the official correspondence in the Department of State of the late Horatio I. [*sic* – J., for Jones] Sprague, who during a record-breaking service of fifty-three years, from 1848 until his death in 1901, had an unusually wide experience in consular affairs, I noticed several reports made by him in 1872–74 in relation to an American derelict vessel, the *Mary Celeste*.
>
> This case, which I have since learned has attracted the attention of fiction writers, both American and English, has appeared to me so extraordinary, by reason of the apparently unfathomable mystery surrounding it, that I here present the facts as gleaned from the official archives ...

Osborne laid out the facts of the affair as punctiliously as a consular official might do. He diverged from the truth by only a few minor aberrations: he put the number of people on the *Mary Celeste* as nine – Capt. Briggs, his wife and daughter, mate Richardson and 'the crew, consisting of five competent and trustworthy seamen' (he seemed to miss out the cook, Edward Head); and stated that 'a child's dress lay upon the sewing-machine as if the mother had stepped out for a moment' at the time of the abandonment. The adventures in Conan Doyle's story 'J. Habakuk Jephson's Statement' were, he assured readers, 'not based upon even a flimsy tissue of fact'.

But Consul Osborne reserved his greatest incredulity for a version of the Hornibrook hypothesis of the great octopus assault. At the same time, he expressed a sense of empathy for the castaways that was largely absent in *Mary Celeste* chronicles up till then:

> The most sensational explanation, however, of the disappearance of the poor souls aboard the *Mary Celeste* which has ever come to my attention was contained in a story in a popular magazine. Retaining the name of the vessel and some of the details, the writer placed the entire ship's company on deck reposing in comfortable chairs, the sea being unusually calm and all hands idle. He then caused an immense sea-serpent to rise out of the depths and after fascinating everyone with its baleful glare the monster deliberately picked one after the

other of its victims off the deck and threw them shrieking into the water. In this way the last person disappeared, leaving nothing to indicate his fate.

Later in the same year, on 16 September 1906, a full-page run-down of the *Mary Celeste* incident was published in the *Washington Times*, of Washington, DC, as part of a series on sea tragedies. Compared with Osborne's almost pristinely factual account, this 'Tragedies of the Sea No. 4: The Mystery of the *Mary Celeste*', was poxed by errors: the brig was 'of New Bedford'; its cargo was 'petroleum and alcohol'; it was commanded by 'Captain Moorhouse', a common misspelling of Morehouse; the derelict was found 'in latitude 36 north', correctly, but in 'longitude 27 west', incorrectly, but another common inaccuracy from the actual '17 degrees west'; the 'Fanny, my dear wife …' note

TRAGEDIES of the SEA No. 4

The MYSTERY of the MARY CELESTE.

'Tragedies of the Sea – No. 4 – The Mystery of the *Mary Celeste*'. (*Washington Times*, 16 September 1906)

found on the log slate; the almost ubiquitous assertion to the effect that, in the galley, 'the coppers were on the stove and meat was prepared for the table'; and an original detail that 'the boat was gone from the stern davits and one of the davits had been broken off'.

A consequence of citing the wrong longitude was that the writer assumed that the distance the *Mary Celeste* had sailed, or drifted, since her last logged position off Santa Maria was only about 35 miles. 'Thus in ten days the brig had drifted only about three and a half miles a day.' In fact, the ship was commonly thought to have sailed at least 380 miles or so with no one on board.

Aside from this litany of commonplace mis-statements, the article was pretty clean and clear, especially concerning the far-fetched stories told about the mysterious abandonment. After the *Mary Celeste* arrived in Gibraltar:

> At once stories began to appear, both in this country and in England, about the *Mary Celeste* and her strange abandonment. None of the stories was wholly true, and some were such wildly constructed fabrications that, while of no value as a record of fact, they made very good romances ... Sweeping aside all the lies and bad guesses of inventive landsmen, and coming down to a basis of reasonable conjecture, the explanation is believed to be this ...

The 'this' was that, assuming the cargo included petroleum with the alcohol, 'in the log of the *Mary Celeste* there appeared, up to the very day of her abandonment, references to rumbling rollings below deck, and the log seemed to indicate a fear among officers and crew that there would be an explosion'. After a particularly 'unusual disturbance' from the cargo, it was thought (by mate Richardson's father) that everyone got off the ship in the boat and expected to head for safety on Santa Maria, but that the boat was swamped by the surf there and everyone drowned. 'Another and very plausible theory' was that they did all get off in the boat, to wait and see what might happen, but that the ship drifted away and left them to their doom.

> These are the probabilities, but still the fate of the *Mary Celeste*'s crew and the reason of their leaving her, all right and tight as she was, is and must continue to be one of the most celebrated mysteries of the sea.

And that was, indeed, as true a conclusion then as it remains today.

Capt. James Henry Winchester's 'Fake News' Obituary

The year 1913 was a benchmark in the embellishment of myth and fiction about the *Mary Celeste*. First out of the traps was the obituary of Capt. James Henry Winchester, who died in East Orange, New Jersey, on 30 January that year. The obituary was mainly about Capt. Winchester's involvement in the *Mary Celeste* mystery. All of it, apart from his general connection with it, was pure invention, especially the suggestion that he was 'enriched' and made 'a fortune' from the salvage prize. The rest was very *Boy's Own*, swashbuckling stuff. Capt. Winchester was born on 4 June 1824 at Annapolis, Nova Scotia. He was 88 years old when he died:

> Capt. Winchester Dead – Man and Boy He Sailed Seas Sixty-four Years – Fortune From Disaster – Enriched by Salvage of the *Marie Celeste*, the Mystery of the Century
>
> Captain James Henry Winchester, one of those old deep sea skippers who live in Joseph Conrad's pages, died here to-day at the ripe age of eighty-nine. Man and boy he had sailed the Seven Seas for sixty-four years – from the time when he ran away, a ten-year-old lad, until he came ashore [i.e., retired] for good and all in 1898 …
>
> Romance and color packed many days of the big, square, old captain's life, but one of the most mysterious incidents connected with this life was the finding of the *Marie Celeste*. A quarter century ago Captain Winchester was beating up the Spanish coast, when he saw a

> large vessel, sailing along with all canvas set. There were no answers to his signals, no replies to his hails, as he drove his ship closer to the mysterious craft.
>
> Finally he put out in a long boat and boarded the *Marie Celeste*, but there was not a soul on board except the cat. No trace of the crew was ever found. Captain Winchester took the ship into port, and the salvage he received made his fortune ...[16]

He found 'the cat'! 'Macavity' lived! Heroic stuff – and balderdash. But a fittingly fictitious fantasy in the mould of the *Mary Celeste* mythosphere.

Right to the end of his life, Capt. Winchester contended that the cause of the *Mary Celeste*'s abandonment was an accumulation of gases from the ship's cargo that threatened an explosion. His grandson, Mr Winchester Noyes, outlined Capt. Winchester's theory to the *Nautical Gazette* in its edition of 24 December 1913, though it included the misinformation that she was 'an American brigantine of 236 tons, built at Bath, Me. [Maine]', and loaded a cargo of 'oil and spirits':

> After leaving port there is no doubt she encountered considerable rough weather, although when picked up it was fine and calm. When boarded by the crew of the *Dei Gratia* one of her hatch covers was found to have been overturned, but the cargo was perfectly intact ...
>
> Captain Winchester ... always held the theory that the cargo had generated vapor and gas, as was entirely probable, from the oil and spirits, during the warm weather voyage particularly. This gas, after a spell of rough weather, caused spontaneous combustion, which one morning suddenly blew off the hatch cover. Seeing the smoke, with the report, and perhaps a flash of flame, and knowing the highly combustible nature of the cargo, the crew made a mad rush for the boat and all hands got safely away, the captain of course taking his chronometer with him.
>
> But the vessel did not burn and there were no more explosions. When the ventilation got to the cargo it cooled off and the *Mary Celeste* kept on her way. She sailed so well alone in fact with a

fair breeze filling her square sails that she ran away from the boat containing the captain and his wife and child and crew. They unfortunately found themselves unable to again reach their vessel and became the victims of another sea tragedy ...

The *Mary Celeste* simply ran away from the boat and the boat or its passengers were never after heard from.

'The Greatest Mystery of the Sea – Can You Solve It?'

The Strand magazine, of London, a popular literary monthly, published an article in July 1913 titled 'The Greatest Mystery of the Sea – Can You Solve It?', which it reprinted from the *Nautical Magazine* of April that year where it ran as 'An Unsolved Mystery', by 'J.S.C.' Four writers of fiction and journalism were invited to offer their proposed solutions to the mystery.

The truth was, though, that the author of the piece himself was quite a fictionist, despite his assertion that 'The circumstances in which the brig *Marie Celeste* was found deserted in mid-ocean are matters of official record, but that only.' 'No trace', it continued, 'of any member of the ship's company of thirteen souls has ever been found. Thirteen, that unlucky number!'

Not to mention untrue. It was the first of a series of wholly invented details about the incident, beginning with the date of her departure from New York ('early in September 1872'), the captain's name ('Captain Ben Griggs'), the vessel's size ('of five hundred tons'), and the ages of his two children ('seven-year-old daughter' and 'twelve-year-old son').

The author imagined the scene on the New York wharf as the '*Marie Celeste*' was loading 'the last article for [the] ship's cabin', the sewing machine belonging to 'Mrs. Griggs', with the captain's wife and children arriving there 'accompanied by the vessel's owner'. The son pleaded to go on the voyage, but the 'owner' commended that he should stay at home and 'stick to his books'.

From that poignant wharf-side vision the author jumped to the scene of the discovery of the abandoned '*Marie Celeste*', warts and all on detail. It claimed to draw on the Department of State's 'official data bearing on the mystery', adding copious dollops of the usual codswallop including a nearby 'tramp steamer' that never was, and a captain and his mate whose names never were – on a brigantine, the *Dei Gratia*, which came out re-rigged as a barque:

> At noon on 5th December, 1872, the Atlantic, at a point three hundred miles due west from Gibraltar, was as smooth as a millpond, and there were three vessels within sight of each other. One was a German tramp steamer holding a course for the West Indies, and crossing the bows of the brig about three miles off. The steamer ran up a signal that called for an answer from the brig. But the brig sent no answer. She was silent ...
>
> The third vessel was the British barque *Dei Gratia*, Captain Boyce, bound for Gibraltar. Captain Boyce, through his telescope, had seen the signal displayed by the tramp steamer when trying to speak to the brig [*sic* – the expression is '*speak* the brig', meaning to contact her]. Also, he had waited in vain for an answering flag from the *Marie Celeste*, the reply demanded by the common code of courtesy on the high seas.
>
> 'Queer, jolly impolite, when I come to think of it,' was the British skipper's comment, and he determined to investigate ...

The 'British skipper', 'Captain Boyce', was, of course, the Nova Scotian Capt. David Morehouse. 'Boyce's' mate was named 'Adams', otherwise factually Oliver Deveau. From this proceeded the fiction that they launched a boat to get over to the '*Marie Celeste*', 'manned by two sailors and carrying both captain and mate from the *Dei Gratia*'. On the deck of the derelict, 'Boyce' and 'Adams' conferred about the possible reasons for her abandonment. 'Capt. Boyce' dismissed them all, after which his mate 'Adams' summarised, adding his own – or rather a version of J.L. Hornibrook's – conjecture:

> 'Well, then, sir, if it weren't mutineers, nor pirates, nor storm, nor wreck, nor leak, nor famine, nor sickness, what could it have been, sir, except a sea-serpent sticking his snout aboard and swallowing 'em up one by one?'

Looking over the ship, they ran through the gamut of discoveries detailed in official records – the blood spots on deck, the bloody sword, the missing chronometer and ship's paper – and from hearsay – the sewing machine in use – but added a few original touches of their own, including a boat still on board. A meal on the captain's table consisted of 'oatmeal, coffee, bacon and eggs' plus the captain's two halves of 'a hard-boiled egg in the shell':

> At another place at the table – probably his wife's – stood a bottle filled with a popular brand of cough medicine. It looked as if the woman's last act aboard the brig had been to remove the cork from the bottle, for the cork lay on the cloth; and, as evidence there had been nothing but a calm sea since the ship was deserted, the narrow tall bottle stood upright close to the edge of the table, not a drop of the medicine having escaped from the bottle.

How the 'small phial of oil for a sewing machine' was transformed into an uncorked bottle of cough medicine is anybody's gue\ss. Conan Doyle's 'J. Habakuk Jephson's Statement' is then mentioned and précised: 'The main features of the yarn are worth repeating as an example of what *might* have happened.' Other possible explanations of 'what *might* have happened' were then laid out by 'other eminent novelists' who were 'good enough to favour us' with their contributions. In the same breath, the magazine invited readers' submissions:

> Whether our readers think that any of them completely solve the mystery, or whether they themselves can suggest something more plausible, now remains to be seen.

The contributing eminences were: Barry Pain (1864–1928), journalist; Morley Roberts (1857–1942), prolific novelist and globe-trotter; Horace Annesley Vachell (1861–1955), writer; and Arthur Morrison (1863–1945), a writer best known for his detective novels.

Vachell's theory was that 'a submarine explosion, of a volcanic character, may have sent to the surface of the Atlantic some lethal gas lighter than water and heavier than air', which 'lingered together for an appreciable time'. The ship's company would have been overwhelmed by the noxious gas, driving them all mad such that they 'plunged into the sea, which swallowed them and their secret'. He admitted, 'I am no chemist, and make these conjectures at hazard.'

Arthur Morrison 'cast his solution into the form of a little story' which occupied the last page and a bit of the article. His 'conjecture' was that a sailor who signed on as 'Joseph Hallers, A.B.' was known as 'Holy Joe', a 'religious crank' who raved about the unlucky number thirteen of the ship's company. The voyage, 'Holy Joe' declaimed, 'started under spiritual portent of great and happy significance' but would end in 'a wholesale conversion and transfiguration' of tragedy. True to his prophecy, the crew were poisoned and either jumped or were thrown overboard by 'Holy Joe', including 'Captain Griggs' and his wife and young daughter. His final act left the ship abandoned to the myths of time:

> With that he spun about and sprang overboard, with the chronometer gripped tight in his arms. The *Marie Celeste* dipped and yawed, took the wind again, and drifted off on the calm Atlantic.

Morley Roberts made a brief statement to the effect that he was sceptical that there was or would ever be any solution. In an article on 'The *Marie Celeste*: Curious Sea Story Recalled', in the Melbourne *Argus* newspaper of 1 November 1919, he advanced the opinion 'that no mystery of either sea or land exceeds in difficulty of solution the story of the *Marie Celeste*'. Furthermore:

> ... he refrains from even thinking of it, because he gets enraged at being unable to offer the maddest guess as to what happened. Therefore, he does not seem to be running a very grave financial risk when he offers £50 to anyone who can produce such a solution of this tantalising puzzle as shellbacks [sailors] would accept as credible.

When Roberts died, on 8 June 1942, aged 85, that £50 'financial risk' almost certainly remained safe, unpaid and part of his estate.

Abel Fosdyk's Story

The premier *Mary Celeste* mystery event of 1913 was a strange story that purported to reveal the truth about the abandonment. It came from the supposed memoirs of a man supposedly named Abel Fosdyk who supposed himself to be the only surviving crew member from that disastrous voyage. His narrative, he said, explained what happened to cause the abandonment of the *Mary Celeste* and appeared as 'a sensational new development' in *The Strand* magazine, in November 1913. The magazine exulted breathlessly that it was 'no less than the discovery of what appears to be a perfectly genuine account of the disaster, left by a survivor!'

The Strand crowed that Abel Fosdyk's narrative (sometimes referred to as 'The Abel Fosdyk Papers') 'brought to light … an account so vivid and alive, so simple and yet so unlikely to be thought of, that one seems to hear the ring of truth on every page'. Over the years that 'ring of truth' which chimed so truly to contemporary readers' ears has become an equally distinct bellwether of the *Mary Celeste* myth.

Abel Fosdyk's narrative came as a document of his personal memoirs that accompanied a letter to *The Strand* sent by a man named as 'Mr. A. Howard Linford, the head master of Peterborough Lodge – Hampstead's largest preparatory school'. Arthur Howard Linford (1861–1945) did indeed establish a prep school of that name in the north London area of Hampstead in 1898. Mr Linford's letter to *The Strand* was apparently written after the magazine's July rendition of the *Mary Celeste* mystery, which Linford was apparently responding to. It ran as follows:

Sir,– A friend has brought to my notice your article on the '*Marie Celeste*.' When I read it the name struck a familiar chord, but I was some days before I could remember under what circumstances I had heard it. At last, however, I recalled an old servant, Abel Fosdyk, committing to my charge, on his death-bed, a quantity of papers contained in three boxes: amongst these he told me would be found the account of [the] *Mary Celeste*. I suppose he said 'the,' but I had at the time no notion of what *Mary Celeste* meant, and imagined it was a woman. I paid but little heed, and merely set the boxes away to a safe keeping, not anticipating they would ever be opened again.

Before commenting on the matter I would like to emphasize the fact that I do not vouch for the truth of anything narrated. No word on the subject was ever mentioned by the writer to me. But the fact that for thirty years he kept not only a diary but also a set of shrewd observations on all that passed, and wrote much and well without our knowing anything of what he was doing, shows him to have been a man of exceptional reticence and self-control.

As for the document, I would rather let it speak for itself; but at the same time I must confess I have been greatly impressed by the following facts: A *brig* called '*Marie* Celeste,' sailing under Captain *Griggs* is under discussion. I find an account of a brigantine named '*Mary* Celeste,' sailing under a Captain *Briggs*. By your courtesy I have now seen the official report, and find in every instance the papers in my possession are correct.

Further, the official papers mention a peculiar damage to the bows and two square cuts on the outside. This, I think, has never till now been made public, yet here again the papers I send you enter most minutely into this alteration of the bows. Finally I find, on inquiry, that the autumn of 1872 was famous for its extraordinary storms in the Atlantic, so much so that a leading article in the *Times* likens it to the period of storms so well known to have prevailed at Cromwell's death. One can easily imagine a captain, working day and night in such conditions, going gradually out of his mind.

> Of course, minute errors will always creep in when relating facts a long time after their occurrence. It is evident to me these facts were written down nearly twenty years after they happened, and no one knows better than myself how easily dates may be forgotten or the sequence of events confused.
>
> A. Howard Linford, MA (Magdalen College, Oxford)
> Peterborough Lodge, Finchley Road, N.W.

Abel Fosdyk's memoir, 'Told In His Own Words', was a handwritten document accompanied, the magazine noted, by sketches drawn by Mr Linford's son, 'then a boy at Harrow – having some artistic gift', which were used to create illustrations for the published narrative. The illustrator was, in fact, a highly proficient and renowned artist of the time, Charles Murray Padday (1868–1954), particularly well known for his maritime scenes. This explains why the drawings he created for the Abel Fosdyk story were of such high quality.

So: to the 'old servant' Abel Fosdyk's yarn:

> It was in the early autumn of 1872 that the *Mary Celeste* sailed out of New York for Europe ... We were bound for Genoa with a cargo of spirits, and I think I might say that no boat of her size – about six hundred tons [*sic*!] – got across the Atlantic that autumn with as little damage as the *Mary Celeste* ...
>
> The party aboard consisted of ten men besides the captain and mate, and, in addition, we carried two passengers in the cabin – viz., the captain's wife, Mrs. Briggs, and 'Baby,' their little girl. Though well beyond those years which would have justified the name, she never went by any other, so far as I can remember ...
>
> I fancy Baby was about seven or eight years old, and as she, as bright and pretty a flower as ever blew in the wind or basked in the sunny plains of life, was indirectly the cause of our disaster, I should like to give a few words of description of her.

Abel Fosdyk's Story.

TOLD IN HIS OWN WORDS.

got across the Atlantic that autumn with as little damage as the Mary Celeste. It was not only the exterior that was good. Everyone on first joining her was struck by the comfort of the foc's'le the light was better by day and by night, there seemed more ventilation and the bunks were wider and longer than usual which to a tall man like myself was a very pleasant discovery

FACSIMILE OF A PORTION OF ABEL FOSDYK'S MS.

IT was in the early autumn of 1872 that the *Mary Celeste*[1] sailed out of New York for Europe. She was as smart a brigantine as one could wish to see, and looked as new as if she had just come out of the maker's hands. We were bound for Genoa with a cargo of spirits, and I think I might say that no boat of her size—about six hundred tons—got across the Atlantic that autumn with as little damage as the *Mary Celeste*. It was not only the exterior that was good. Everyone on first joining her was struck by the comfort of the fo'c's'le. The light was better by day and by night, there seemed more ventilation, and the bunks were wider and longer than usual, which, to a tall man like myself, was a very pleasant discovery. In fact, if only the men in the fo'c's'le had had their instincts in the matter of vermin less morbidly sportsmanlike, it would have been almost as good as being in the cabin itself. Curiously, I had intended this to be my last voyage in her, though not owing to the reasons which necessitated my secreting myself later, but because my sister—my only relative—had just died and I did not wish to return to America for some time. I had also another and more private reason.[2]

The party aboard consisted of ten men besides the captain and mate, and, in addition, we carried two passengers in the cabin—viz., the captain's wife, Mrs. Briggs,[3] and "Baby," their little girl. Though well beyond those years which would have justified the name, she never went by any other, so far as I can remember. Moreover, she gave me (or rather her mother did) a portrait of herself

"BABY" AT THE AGE OF TWO.

(This is the portrait given by

[1] The ship is called in the official records the *Marie Celeste*, the *Mary Celeste*

[2] No doubt these reasons for secrecy at the time were also those which caused him to keep silence after the disaster.

[3] The captain's name is given in our original account as Griggs. It appears, however, from the official report that his name was Briggs, so that the present writer is quite accurate. It appears, also, from other papers left by the writer that he was engaged rather as a steward than as a sailor, his special duty being to attend on

Abel Fosdyk's Story. (*The Strand*, November 1913)

This he proceeded to do. Afterwards he identified some of the crew, 'taking the fo'c's'le as a starting point', meaning the common sailors amongst the crew who bunked up there:

> Joe, who was ship's carpenter, had the bunk above me, and Robin, so-called, I believe, because he had a curious red-fronted jersey, in the next to me, whilst Fred and Ginger – whose real name, I fancy, was Odell – and the boy had the three corresponding on the opposite side.

Abel Fosdyk identified the next in the line-up, a young black lad – whom he thought 'was a stowaway' – by a name and in terms that were common currency in the lingo of the time but which are certainly not legal tender and are indeed highly offensive in the parlance of today:

> At any rate, I quite well remember Captain Briggs, who evidently was under the impression we were thirteen on board, whereas we were fourteen, saying to the man at the wheel …: 'If I hear any more nonsense about thirteen being an unlucky number, I'll jolly well knock your head off, and then we shall be twelve.'

The voyage started well with fine weather. After five days, though, it turned stormy. Capt. Briggs was on deck 'incessantly':

> Day after day the waves roared and hissed and boomed upon our sides – at one moment we were on a huge crest, at the next deep down between walls of water which looked each moment as though they would engulf us; the winds howled and whistled in the rigging; the dull, grey, leaden-looking clouds chased each other over the sky.
>
> Each dawn revealed the same monotonous picture, each sunset left it still unchanged. The nights were even worse than the days, for darkness added so much to the difficulties of moving about and of keeping a look-out.

ABEL FOSDYK'S STORY. 489

Drawn by C. M. Padday.

"ON THE BOWSPRIT, WITHOUT HOLDING ON TO ANYTHING, STOOD BABY."

Abel Fosdyk's Story: 'Baby' on *Mary Celeste*'s bowsprit. (*The Strand*, November 1913)

> This awe-inspiring weather continued, practically without intermission, for about a month. I heard the captain say one day to the mate that in all his experience of the sea he had never known such a continuous series of gales as we had during the latter half of October and the first half of November.

Although the ship 'was perfect', the stormy weather took its toll on the captain, who went 'almost without sleep throughout the time'. The strain got to him: 'his nerves had got into such a state that he was now so irritable one scarcely dared approach him'. Mrs Briggs, 'usually a robust woman', suffered equally from sea-sickness. She was often 'violently sick and growing daily thinner and paler'. Eventually she 'succumbed and could no longer get about'. She took to her bed 'for quite a fortnight' and reappeared looking 'but the shadow of her former self'.

"BABY" ON HER QUARTER-DECK.
(Drawn from a sketch made under the writer's direction.)

Abel Fosdyk's Story: 'Baby' on the platform. (*The Strand*, November 1913)

So, things were not going well for the *Mary Celeste*, to say the least, when, getting into calm weather, Abel Fosdyk described 'two interesting events'.

The first was when Capt. Briggs, exceedingly irritable and well out of sorts by then, saw 'Baby' standing on the bowsprit 'without holding on to anything'. For that he scolded the girl severely, 'boxed her ears soundly and sent her, crying her eyes out, below'. He then, possibly somewhat ashamed about his harsh treatment of his daughter, ordered the carpenter to knock up 'a little barricade by the bowsprit' that the girl would be safe sitting on in fine weather. The platform was known as 'Baby's quarter-deck'.

The second event was that they encountered the hull of a capsized ship, 'what looked at first like a dead whale'. Four men were clinging to the hull. Taking a boat over to investigate, they discovered that 'on nearer inspection it was apparent that one man was dead, and even decomposed'. So, too, were two others, while a fourth was still alive.

With considerable difficulty they got the barely surviving man into the boat. 'His face was badly cut and much swollen, and one hand and arm were terribly lacerated; two joints of the little finger and the third finger were torn off, and the bone protruded about half an inch.' Berthed in the ship to recover, the man revealed only his name, 'Ebenezer', and added 'Bristol' before he died during the night and was committed to the deep the next morning:

> Those that go down to the sea in ships must needs see strange sights, and few are stranger than the solemn burying in the sea of an unknown man who had come into our lives only to pass out again, and more than one even jested on the fact. Had they but known how soon they, too, would go down into those unknown depths to lie until the last trump should sound, they might, perhaps, have been less inclined to frivolity and more to sober contemplation.

Capt. Briggs declined further 'in such a state of nervous breakdown that no owner would have entrusted his ship to him for five minutes'.

One night, they observed 'something awful happening in the sky' – an intense meteor shower, like some portent of what was to come a few days later: 'the final catastrophe'.

In the cabin one day during calm weather, the mate, Harry, claimed to Capt. Briggs that 'a man can't swim in his clothes'. The captain, indignant at the remark, repeated, 'A – man – can't – swim – in – his – clothes?' He was determined to show that *he* could certainly 'swim in his clothes' by swimming around the ship fully clothed. A few of the crew, at Mrs Briggs' request, swam with him in case anything happened to her husband. As everyone on board crowded on to 'Baby's quarterdeck' to watch the swimmers come round the bow of the ship, the platform collapsed, spilling them all into the water.

Abel Fosdyk's Story: Collapse of 'Baby's' platform. (*The Strand*, November 1913)

Abel Fosdyk's Story: Appearance of a shark. (*The Strand*, November 1913)

Abel floated on the wreckage of the platform with a barely live man clinging to it, who 'towards evening ... moved, sighed, and slipped into the water', dead. The rest of the crew drowned, as did the captain, Mrs Briggs and 'Baby'. Or some might have been taken by a shark which appeared between the wrecked platform and the hull of the ship. Eventually, as the ship drifted away in a rising breeze with no one left on board:

> No signs of the captain could be seen, nor of anyone else. I was alone upon the waste of waters. I had never realized before what 'alone' really meant, and it is a feeling, when once realized, that no language can describe.

Abel Fosdyk drifted as a castaway on the platform-raft for many days. Finally he washed ashore on a beach. Awakening from his delirium, he saw 'a black man stooping beside me, pouring water into my mouth'. He was, he wrote, rescued by 'three blacks and a dark European and his wife, talking Heaven only knows what language':

> I only discovered afterwards that it was on the north-west coast of Africa that I had landed, and there I remained, suffering all the while from spasmodic pains. After some weeks a small sailing-boat, which had evidently been expected, arrived. There was much pointing to me and excited gesticulation, and finally I went on board and got to Algiers. From here I worked to and from Marseilles for several months, but always feeling wretchedly ill. Finally I was taken very ill at Marseilles and went into the hospital, where an operation was performed, from which, when I recovered, I quickly gained my former health.
>
> About four months later, or in the summer of 1874, I came to England and met in the Surrey Commercial Dock [London] the man who introduced me to my late employer, in whose service ashore I remained until he died, and in the service of whose son I still am, and I pray God I may remain so until it pleases Him to take me home.

[Note by the writer's employer: 'A pious wish which the Almighty saw fit to grant to a trustworthy and much-tried man.']

The introductory paragraph of 'The Greatest Mystery of the Sea: Can You Solve It?', in *The Strand*'s July issue, had commended readers to take up their pens and try their hand at solving the mystery:

> It is possible that the explanation of this strange mystery is really quite simple, and if some plausible solution should occur to any of our readers we shall be very glad to hear from them, and to publish and pay for anything we decide to use.

Mr. A. Howard Linford of Peterborough Lodge school up in north London must have chortled at the challenge, gleefully uncorked a bottle of his creative juices, and taken a deep swig before composing 'Abel Fosdyk's Story, In His Own Words' – pocketing the magazine's shilling for the publication of his ably crafted 'solution'.

The *Nautical Gazette*, of New York, in its 17 December issue of 1913, gave a caustic review of the Abel Fosdyk story as 'pure fiction'. It subjoined the equally caustic assessment by a 'retired mariner':

> The fellow who wrote that doesn't know a poopdeck from a jib-downhaul. Anything does for a sea yarn.
>
> The farther you get from the truth the better it takes with those who don't know the difference.

R.E. Greenhough's 'Message-in-a-Bottle' Story

At around the same time as Mr Linford's prize-winning Abel Fosdyk exposé appeared, and apparently in response to it, a merchant seaman named R.E. Greenhough, 2nd officer in the steamship *Tortuguero* in the Liverpool docks at the time, wrote a letter to the *Liverpool Weekly Mercury* published on 7 November 1913.

In his letter, dated 31 October 1913, Greenhough claimed that he had a written account which, he said, came into his hands 'in a strange manner' some years before and which explained an alternative version of the mystery of the *Mary Celeste*. He was clearly familiar with the various conjectures and suppositions written about the incident:

> I read with surprise that the reasons which led to her [*Mary Celeste*'s] desertion, and the ultimate fate of her crew, were matters of conjecture only. Nor could any reason, theoretical or otherwise, be given to explain why the crew of the brig should depart so hurriedly and disappear from human ken … I will now relate certain happenings, which will, I think, convince you of the truth of the solution.
>
> It was, I think, at the end of the year 1904 (I am not sure of the date – it may have been in the spring of 1905 – I cannot remember now, having taken no particular note of the time) that I was serving as apprentice on the barque *Ardorinha*. She was a Swansea [Wales] vessel then, although I believe she has been sold to Mr. A.D. Borde, of Nantes. We were bound out to Chili with coal.

So far, so good – apart from the name of the barque: there was none of that name at that time, but there *was* a big (3,200 tons) four-masted Swansea barque named *Andorinha*. (To be fair, a single misplaced letter of a ship's name in the press wasn't terribly unusual in those days.) The *Andorinha* did leave Port Talbot, near Swansea, towards the end of 1904 on a voyage to Taltal, in northern Chile, to pick up a cargo of nitrate, used at the time as a fertiliser. *Andorinha* sailed from Chile on her return voyage to Britain in April 1905: in other words, in the northern hemisphere spring of that year. And she *was* in fact sold to the French shipping company A.D. Bordes of Nantes, in Brittany, in 1909, and renamed *Hélène*.

So the story being recounted by Greenhough was plausible enough, as far as it went. He continued that the ship eventually 'had a succession of flat, windless days, and [we] were drifting at the will of the currents'. This was, recognisable by the continuation of his narrative, near the desolate Saint Peter and Saint Paul Archipelago off the north-east coast of Brazil, just 1 degree north of the equator. This volcanic clutch of islets was on the usual route of sailing ships in those days bound from northern Europe to the west coast of South America via Cape Horn:

> I well remember how, in the early morning, we sighted a group of small islands about four miles distant, towards which the vessel was slowly drifting helplessly, but not with any danger, as the set of the current would take her clear of them. I asked the boatswain if he knew what islands they were.
>
> 'St. Paul's Rocks,' he said. 'Desert islands. Top of a mountain stickin' out of the --- water. Many a ship has gone to --- there of a dark night.' This was the substance of his remarks as far as I remember them.

Greenhough proceeded to relate that the mate ordered a boat to be taken ashore to obtain some sand, 'which he used for scrubbing the decks', and that he 'thought himself lucky to be one of the crew picked on that occasion' to go in the boat. On shore they found plenty of guano – the hardened deposits of seagull droppings, also used as nitrogen fertiliser – but no sand.

Their other discovery was the source of the *Mary Celeste* account that came into apprentice Greenhough's hands 'in a strange manner':

> Propped up, in the shade of a high peak on the island, under a shelving rock, we found the skeleton of a man, his bones, bleached snow white, some sailor, his ship wrecked and sunk, had crawled here to die.

They threw the skeleton into the sea 'for burial'. Greenhough meanwhile:

> ... picked up a bottle from under the rocks, where the bones had rested. It was stuffed with soiled and faded papers. I thought it may be an account of buried treasure, a chart or something of that kind. I stowed it in my pocket, without remarking about it.

Later that night he broke the bottle, with 'breathless eagerness', to reveal the treasure message, only to discover several sheets of paper, 'partly mouldy and damp-stained as to be quite illegible, written in German'. Since no one on board knew German, he stuffed the papers into his sea chest and forgot about them.

Towards the end of 1909, he wrote, he was 2nd officer on a tramp steamer, 'loading grain at Rosario', in Argentina. A German who was tallying the loading of the grain and who 'spoke perfect English' obliged him one day with a translation of the bottle papers, 'as much as he could', found by the side of the 'bleached snow white' skeleton years before.

The translation started:

> I am dying. My ship struck these rocks at dawn three days ago. She sank immediately. Only I of all her crew reached this shore alive. There is no water; I am dying of thirst. It has been a voyage of disaster. Fate has been against me all through.

> I was master and part-owner of the ship. We (Here the writing has disappeared from half a page.) the second engineer. Killed in the engine-room. Three deaths in two days. Then came the poison on the seventh day out. I can blame no one for this. It was the food was bad. Noon all were well, midnight some were dead, the others nigh to it. I do not (Many words missing.) I wish I had (Missing.) two days.
>
> I went to seek the others. Ship had stopped. Fires out. Nearly all were dead, only six alive. Mate, engineer, two firemen, one sailor …

The chronometer, the message said, 'had run down' because the writer, 'in [his] agony', forgot to wind it, the 'only one on ship':

> It was the final catastrophe. Ship helpless, Too weak to get steam on boilers. And so for three days we lay. Knew must seek assistance to take us to Gibraltar for crew. That was ruin. Ship not insured. If English found cargo it was prison and confiscation.

Eventually they got steam up and headed for Lisbon. On the way:

> Early morning sighted small brig becalmed. I took little note of her. Mate said, 'Take her crew.' It was the devil's voice.

Some of the men boarded the becalmed brig:

> Captain asked why we came. His wife and child were with him. It was hard. It would have been easy without the woman. But the mate got behind the captain, he and two others, and threw him. His wife fainted. Then we pointed pistols. Crew went into the boats quietly. One man shot. He fell into the sea. It (Some words missing.) took chronometer and ship's papers, and then we went back to my ship. We left no one on board.
>
> The brig was called *Marie Celeste*. Would to God I had never seen her. Then the child would be yet alive. I cannot forget the child.

The captain, his wife and the little girl, together with the mate from the abandoned '*Marie Celeste*', were now on board the steamer 'with the brig's chronometer'. The steamer captain asked the mate what error the chronometer had, a common bit of information needed for the accurate navigation of ships. But what he said 'was wrong':

> At noon the day we struck [the rocks] the chronometer put us to pass thirty miles off these rocks ... She sank at once, almost with the crash, into deep water. I heard a great cry, and a shriek of the child ... Shark caught her. I hear her cry still. I have murdered that little child.
>
> I reached the shore and lay until dawn. I was alone; all the others dead. I was mad with grief, then with thirst. Now, thank God, I am dying. I am writing this in my notebook. I wonder ... a great crime. The need was great, but, O God, the child. It lies ... in a little bottle I found washed ashore. It will keep it dry in the rainy season ...
>
> I can write no more.

And so the bottle message narrative ended 'as my German friend translated it'. Greenhough surmised that 'this steamer was engaged in a trade requiring secrecy. What her name was or where she was bound is not stated.' The faulty chronometer, he believed, was 'feasible enough, and undoubtedly led to the foundering of the steamer'.

All the details of Greenhough's narrative were, in fact, reasonably plausible – some, possibly, even true. But sailors in days of yore were much inclined to spin salty yarns, especially if they were spliced, diced and spiced with real events they were familiar with.

Certain particulars in the bottle message Greenhough claimed to have found beside the skeleton on St Paul's Rocks resonated with the *Mary Celeste* events of 1872. But they chimed just as clearly with fictions in more recent published accounts that he had already read or perhaps heard about: the German tramp steamer from *The Strand* article of July 1913, with the addition of a piratical kidnapping of the *Mary Celeste* people by the steamer's men; the part-ownership of the steamer by her late skeletal master, the author of the bottle message, as Capt. Briggs had been part-owner and master of the *Mary Celeste*; the supposed violence on board the *Mary Celeste*; the Gibraltar and Lisbon links; the missing chronometer; and the shark that, with 'a great cry, and shriek of the child', took her when his ship foundered on St Paul's Rocks, from Abel Fosdyk's story of the collapsed platform and drowned swimmers.

Another fiction from earlier sources was that 'all the boats' on the *Mary Celeste* were in place on the ship when she was found abandoned. The piratical abduction of the ship's company by the presumably German steamer of Greenhough's yarn would have left the boats in place, according with their mythical presence on board.

As Greenhough wrote about the missing bits in the message, the truth of the story was as leaky as the imagination was necessary to caulk it:

> The broken threads of the story can only be filled in by imagination. I make no attempt to do it. I have written the translation as it was given to me. Of the truth of it I leave others to judge.

The appearance of a German tramp steamer in the distance when the *Dei Gratia* came upon the *Mary Celeste* held sway in the mythosphere as a staple fiction for many years. It popped up in a long article from *The Herald* newspaper, of Melbourne, on 18 March 1937, '*Marie Celeste* Baffles the World', in its 'Great Dramas of the Sea' series. It almost incidentally misidentified the *Dei Gratia*, not for the first time, as a barque. And the weather it portrayed was far from the actual conditions of a northerly breeze and sloppy chop of seas:

> It was a fine morning in the Atlantic on December 5, 1872. The sea was remarkably smooth, the wind slight and variable. Plugging across to Gibraltar was the barque *Dei Gratia*, of Nova Scotia. Toward her came a German tramp, bound for the West Indies. Between them lay a brigantine, sails set, behaving in the most curious manner ...

> So oddly did she move that both the barque and the German tramp signalled her. No answering signal came from the brigantine. The tramp shrugged her untidy shoulders and passed on towards the West Indies.

'Untidy shoulders': a neat characterisation of a *tramp* steamer. The rest of the reconstruction of events was riddled with the usual concoction of dicey details. The author, however, seemed quite satisfied with his rendition: 'Those, then, are the facts of the mystery of the *Marie Celeste*.' Well, some were, and some weren't – a rather typical hotchpotch of fact, fiction and fantasy, though with the definitive and concluding truth that:

> The mystery of the *Marie Celeste* must remain a mystery, irritating though that thought may be.

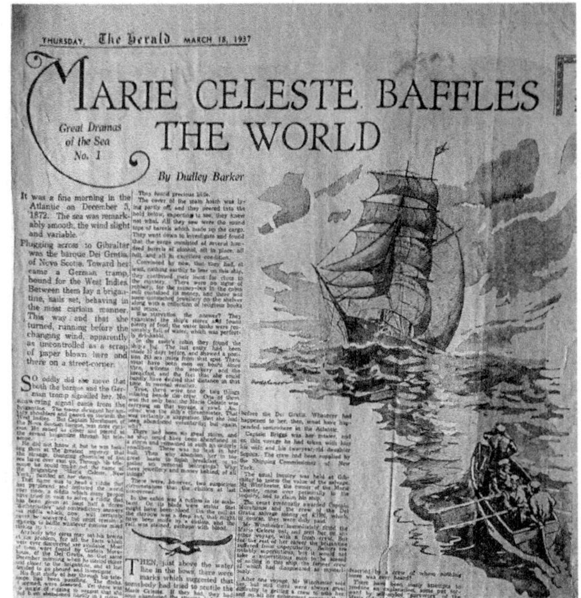

THURSDAY, The Herald MARCH 18, 1937

MARIE CELESTE BAFFLES THE WORLD

Great Dramas of the Sea No. 1

By Dudley Barker

It was a fine morning in the Atlantic on December 5, 1872. The sea was remarkably smooth, the wind slight and variable.

Plugging across to Gibraltar was the barque Dei Gratia, of Nova Scotia. Toward her came a German tramp, bound for the West Indies. Between them lay a brigantine, sails set, behaving in the most curious manner. This way and that she turned, running before the changing wind, apparently as uncontrolled as a scrap of paper blown here and there on a street-corner.

SO oddly did she move that both the barque and the German tramp signalled her. No answering signal came from the brigantine.

They found precious little.

The enduring and baffling mystery of the *Mary Celeste*. (*The Herald* [Melbourne], 18 March 1937)

Captain Lukhmanoff's Story

Stories of piratical assault upon the *Mary Celeste* seemed to be the *plat du jour* of 1913. The December issue of the *Nautical Magazine* published a narrative 'forwarded [to it] by Captain D. Lukhmanoff, the well-known agent of the Russian Volunteer Fleet at Hong Kong'. The story, it said, 'was related to him by an old Greek sailor on board the Italian brig *Ozama*, in 1884'.

The Russian Volunteer Fleet was established at St Petersburg in 1878 under the aegis of Czar Alexander III and supported by voluntary contributions, hence the name. It was characterised as a 'Patriotic Squadron' of armed merchant ships after the Russo-Turkish War of 1877–78. Since the war had ended by then, the ships were employed mainly for peacetime passenger and cargo transport, particularly in the Pacific Far East. Its base there was at Nagasaki, Japan. And there *was* an agent thereabouts named D.A. Lukhmanoff who might feasibly have been at Hong Kong at some point.

Capt. Lukhmanoff was almost 50 years old when his story appeared in the *Nautical Magazine*. It concerned events from 1884 when he had just finished his apprenticeship at the age of 18, almost thirty years before:

> After finishing my apprenticeship, I signed on at Genoa in the beginning of June, 1884, as an ordinary seaman in the Italian brig *Ozama*, bound to the West Indies ... In the middle of July – the exact date I don't remember now – we passed Gibraltar and entered the Atlantic ...
>
> The weather was beautiful, and light winds allowed us to carry all sails. The ocean was smooth and its deep blue colour rivalled with

> the cloudless sky. The only disagreeable things on board were bad food and the bad and offensive treatment of the crew. I, as a beginner and foreigner, got the worst of it, but very soon I found the powerful patronage of one old sailor.

Novice Ordinary Seaman Lukhmanoff's 'patronage' ally was 'a Greek from Mitylene, named Demetrius Specioti' of almost 60 years of age, 'while I was only eighteen'. Specioti was 'an old sea-dog and a man of great strength', and 'one of the most esteemed men on board'. This 'old sea-dog' entertained the young Lukhmanoff during peaceful night watches on deck with yarns of his seafaring life. Half a lifetime later:

> Now when I read in the *Nautical Magazine* the story about the enigmatic disappearance of the crew of the *Marie Celeste*, the image of old Specioti swam out from the dense fog of my memory, and to the smallest detail I recollected one of his stories which dealt with the mysterious disappearance of the *Marie Celeste*'s crew. He told it to me one lovely calm night, on the fifth or sixth day after our passing Gibraltar.
>
> I was on the lookout at that moment. Specioti silently stepped on the foc'sle-head and took a seat on the cat-head. He was silent for a long time smoking his short clay pipe and looking attentively into the dark sea. At last he grumbled through his nose: 'Damned place, damned brig!' And in a fainter tone, hardly audible to me, '*Marie Celeste*! *Marie Celeste*!'

Old Specioti swore young Lukhmanoff to secrecy about the story he was about to spin to him. If he broke the confidence, he, Lukhmanoff, would 'fly overboard on the first dark night'. Refreshing his pipe with tobacco, Specioti revealed that, after almost sixty years and a life of hard work, he 'had nothing; no home, no family, no money, neither good clothes, and do you know why? Because God has punished me for my former love of gain and manslaughter.' Referring to the story he was about to tell, Specioti moralised that:

> 'It matters not if they were bad men, but God does not allow a man to kill another. Man has no right to take from the other man the things which he cannot return; only God has a power over man's life!'

He had been, he said, a wealthy man some fifteen years before, from what he had earned 'by sailing on board the American clippers and to say true also on board the slavers'. He bought a small tavern in Boston; married a much younger girl who eventually 'ran away with a young American cowboy'; in his despair, drink and dice ruined him; and, with 'less than a hundred dollars' from the sale of his pub, went back to seafaring.

At New York he signed on an American brig where 'life was very good'. The captain was 'a jolly and noble man' who 'sailed together with his wife and a little daughter'. One morning, 'bound to the Mediterranean', they sighted a brig similar to their own:

> 'It happened not very far from Gibraltar, and might be at the same place as where we are now. It was a dead calm, and both vessels remained motionless, only slightly rolling on the sea. After the sunrise, a gentle breeze arose and about seven o'clock in the morning we came closer to each other; afterwards the breeze fell down again.'

The other brig hoisted the English flag and the signal: 'Short of provisions – Starving'. They launched a boat to get to the American brig. The man at the tiller was 'a dark-faced man with a long beard, wearing a sombrero and red jersey'. As soon as the boat was tied alongside, 'the tarpaulin arose from the bottom of the boat and six or seven men with revolvers in hands jumped from below'. The 'brigands' climbed aboard 'and stood over us with revolvers in their hands'.

The 'swarthy-faced one' explained, quite reasonably but no less ruthlessly, that he was short of crew. He needed the American brig's men to come on board his own vessel, where they would get 'good pay and will be satisfied'. Any of them resisting his enticements would be shot, a fairly persuasive inducement to obey. The captain came along, too, with his wife and daughter. Last to board was 'the dark-faced' leader of the brigand-brig who carried the chronometer and ship's papers from the now abandoned American brig.

On board the 'English' brig, Specioti immediately realised that she was a 'slaver', from the ring-bolts screwed to her deck by which slaves were bound for punishments meted out to them. Specioti described the captain who had stayed on board his ship and now walked down from the after-deck:

> 'He was a tall, thin-bodied man in a Panama hat and white jacket. His face was clean-shaved and rather reddish than dark. Big eagle nose and deep-placed cold grey eyes under grey hanging eyebrows, giving him the appearance of a free will, cruel and rapacious man. He fixed his eyes on us and spoke with a stiffish and metallic voice with a good English accent. "The fever has carried away half of my men. When our boat went after you, I remained alone on board. You must help me. Your captain will act as my chief mate; he need not be afraid of his wife and girl, they will be placed together with him in the same cabin. Your mate will act as my boatswain, as the second mate I have" – and he pointed with his hand to the dark-faced brigand in red jersey – "all the rest of you will work as my sailors. Your future is in your own hands and fully depends on your behaviour on board of my ship." With these last words he turned back and went aft.'

As the breeze strengthened, the abandoned brig 'dropped under the horizon and on the next morning she was no longer seen'. For the next few weeks, Specioti narrated, the fever 'carried off one victim after another', the first being 'the girl, her mother and our good old captain'. As they buried bodies nearly every day into the sea, 'the sharks were always pursuing our ship'.

On 'a starry but moonless night', as the ship sailed south-west further into the Atlantic, the remaining seven kidnapped crew hatched a plan to overwhelm and kill the remaining seven Spaniards of the slaver brig. Specioti would first finish off the captain as he slept on a chair on the after-deck by smashing his head in with an iron capstan bar. He would then whistle that the deed was done as a signal that his shipmates could 'finish the rest':

> 'My heart was beating awfully when I, with the capstan bar in hands, went to kill a sleeping man. It was against all my nature, but there was nothing else to do, and to cut it short, I killed the captain and gave the whistle. Suddenly at that moment there happened something unexplainable. There was a horrible crash and shock of such a force that I fell down. Pieces of spars rushed down on the deck and our brig fell on her port side. A big ocean steamer cut our brig nearly into two, which was according to her fashion sailed without lights.'

The steamer's crew entreated them to climb over to them:

> 'But nobody answered and nobody climbed over from the brig. The steamer's bow smashed the side of the brig to pieces where the crew were sleeping on deck and where after my whistle began the bloody assassination'.

Only Specioti amongst his shipmates managed to leap on to the steamer's bow. The rest drowned as the brig fell on her side: 'her stern rose up for a moment and then disappeared'. Eventually the steamer landed Specioti at her destination of Genoa, though he was a troubled man:

> 'But the heavy thought that I had killed a man and that after my whistle the other men killed six more, really made me a lunatic!'

He eventually recovered and, as he told young Lukhmanoff, he was 'still all right and still a sailor'. But he had no money. Lukhmanoff asked why not, to which Specioti revealed the penance of his secret guilt:

> 'Well, why not, if you want I will tell you. I ordered in the monasteries masses for the dead and that costs money.' With these words,

old Specioti rose up from the cat-head and silently went down from the forecastle.

Thus ended Capt. Lukhmanoff's story of 'old Specioti's' narrative of how his ship, the '*Marie Celeste*! *Marie Celeste*!', was seized by a piratical band of brigands and abandoned, leaving only the flotsam of his salt-seasoned yarn afloat.

Captain Lucy's Story

The spate of fictions about the *Mary Celeste* that appeared in 1913, and before, then dried up for about ten years. She slunk out of the public eye until a new story similar in style to the Lukhmanoff account surfaced in a London newspaper in 1924. A certain Capt. H. Lucy, 'whose name is respected all over the Mediterranean and in Eastern waters', like agent Lukhmanoff's renown in the Far East, claimed he was 'the only man living who knows how the *Marie Celeste* was abandoned'.

The claim was that 'he heard the story 42 years ago [i.e., in 1882], under oath not to divulge it till his informant had died'. With his 'informant' by then presumably dead, Lucy believed he was 'now ... at liberty to speak'.

The so-called 'Captain H. Lucy' was apparently 70 years old. He apparently fought in the Dardanelles in the First World War, was apparently shot in the leg and joined the Italian Navy, and, to ice the cake of his reputation, apparently received both France's Croix de Guerre and 'the Italian Cross of Merit'. Many of the latter Italian honours were awarded. Of the far fewer French medals, there is no mention of a 'Lucy', captain or otherwise, amongst the archives.

Lucy related that around the beginning of September 1924 he turned up in London from 'his home in India' to unburden himself to the press of his *Mary Celeste* yarn, 'the real solution of the mystery of the *Marie Celeste*', as the newspapers crowed:

> 'I heard the true story of the *Marie Celeste* when I was mate of the Island Princess, cruising in the South Seas,' said Captain Lucy. 'It was told to me under oath by a man called Trigg whom I had met

in the Bay View Hotel, Melbourne, and for whom I found a job as bos'n of our Kanaka crew.

'This man Trigg – though I am sure it was an assumed name – had been bos'n of the Marie Celeste. I only learned this after living in the same ship with him for three months. Bit by bit he told me the story, which I will tell you in his own words – as near as I can remember:-'

Informant Trigg took the stage:

> "I signed on as bos'n of the *Marie Celeste* at Boston," Trigg told me. "We loaded in New York for Genoa in 1872. We made good sailing across the Atlantic and expected to pick up the coast of Portugal within the next 24 hours. About midday we sighted a steamer and, as she rolled to port and starboard and seeing no one aboard, we concluded she was a derelict."'

On a calm sea Trigg, the mate, 'and four others' rowed across to board the stranger, 'on the chance of finding something useful'. The name of the steamer had apparently been rusted away by salt water, though they could see that 'she belonged to the Port of London'. They found 'a large iron safe' on board 'in the purser's cabin'. Unable to open it, Trigg and another man rowed back to the '*Marie Celeste*' to summon the carpenter, who brought over a bag of tools.

> '"We found the safe contained about £3,500 in gold and silver … I went back and told Captain Briggs, who at once came over to the derelict. The captain had a few private words with the mate, and it was decided to take the money aboard the *Marie Celeste*, which we did in the boats belonging to the derelict steamer. Before we left, however, the captain told the carpenter to go below and open out one of the watercocks and sink the ship, as she was a danger to shipping."'

The booty from the steamer's safe was divvied up: £1,200 to Capt. Briggs, £600 to the chief mate, £400 to the second mate, £300 to

Trigg, and the remaining £1,000 'equally divided between the crew, who were all quite satisfied'. A communal guilty awareness that 'by taking the money we had done an illegal act' persuaded Capt. Briggs that they should 'sink the *Marie Celeste* and make for Cadiz' on the southern coast of Spain. That idea was scuppered by the appearance of another vessel, which made them concerned 'there would be a suspicion of foul play':

> '"We then decided to get away from the *Marie Celeste* in the three boats which belonged to the sunk steamer. We painted these boats with the name of a schooner belonging to London, put our boxes in the boats with the money and some food and water. There was then a north-east wind blowing. This accounted for the course the deserted *Marie Celeste* was on when sighted by the British barque, which took her into Gibraltar."'

At Cadiz the following day they 'reported the loss of the schooner' to the authorities and then 'split up'. Some went to London 'by a Spanish fruit boat'. Trigg, together with Capt. Briggs, his wife and daughter, and the two mates, went to Marseilles. Eventually Trigg went on to Australia. There Capt. Lucy bumped into him, took him on as 'bos'n' (boatswain) and heard 'this strange story of the sea', which he kept to himself 'for something like 42 years':

> 'That,' said Captain Lucy, 'is the story told me by this man Trigg. I believe it to be the only true story of the *Marie Celeste*. I saw his papers, which proved that he signed on at Boston aboard the *Marie Celeste*, but I must say that he always covered up his name when he showed it to me. I also believe Trigg knew the name of the derelict from which they took the money, but he never trusted me sufficiently to tell.
>
> 'I naturally made private inquiries about him for my own satisfaction, and discovered that he had about £100 in the Bank of Australia. I also discovered that he had lived at the Bay View Hotel, King

> Street, Melbourne, for about five years, without being known to do any work.'

Truth be told, the putative Capt. Lucy's account of the supposed Trigg memoir as 'the only true story of the *Marie Celeste*' hardly aspired to, much less reached, the literary merit of Conan Doyle's 'J. Habakuk Jephson's Statement'. It was peppered with grains of truth but far more liberally dosed with pinches of salt.

Kathleen Woodward, a writer for the *New York Times*, summarised the story in a piece published by the newspaper on 12 October 1924 under the title 'Mystery Of The *Marie Celeste*'. She included her summary of the Abel Fosdyk story, which she thought was 'a good story – and plausible in part', but which was 'finally discredited on certain points, and passed into the limbo of the *Marie* myths and traditions'.

Her own summary of the *Mary Celeste* mystery voyage leaked with a profusion of 'certain points', such as that she had 'a crew of seventeen', that 'she was found by a Captain Boyce of the British brigantine *Dei Gratia*', that 'not one of her boats was missing', that there was the much-storied 'half-eaten meal' on the cabin table, that the *Dei Gratia* towed the *Mary Celeste* into Gibraltar, and so on.

Woodward's piece ended with the end of Capt. Lucy's narrative. She remained silent on its veracity, 'in limbo' but for her editor's assessment of it as the sub-heading of the article: 'Perhaps the True Story of a Ship's Company Vanished Half a Century Ago.'

Or not. Dr Oliver Warren Cobb, of Easthampton, Massachusetts, was a cousin of both Capt. Benjamin Briggs and his wife Sarah Elizabeth (*née* Cobb). He authored the family memoir *Rose Cottage* (published in 1940), took a keen interest in the *Mary Celeste* mystery over many years and offered one of the most plausible solutions for it (having been a deep-sea mariner in his younger years). He wrote a letter to the *New York Times* (26 October 1924) upbraiding Kathleen Woodward's account in its multitude of mis-statements, and offered that:

It is not necessary to introduce fiction or add to the mystery of the story. On board a whaler, or maybe a trader among the islands of the Pacific, or it may be on a transatlantic liner, a sailor in the forecastle or an officer on the bridge will light his pipe and after two or three puffs of smoke will say, 'Well, what do you suppose ever became of the crew of the *Marie Celeste*?'

Fifty-two years have passed and still the question and no real answer.

John Pemberton's Story

In the 26 July 1926 issue of *Chambers's Journal*, a piece written by a certain Lee Kaye purported to tell 'The Truth About *Marie Celeste*: A Survivor Story'. It began:

> Here follows the true story of the brig *Marie Celeste*, and an exact and complete explanation of the mystery which has hung round her name.

What followed was a preface of 'the plain facts as recorded by the captain of the finding vessel', the *Dei Gratia*'s Capt. Morehouse. These were mainly as fanciful as the cat he said was found 'sleeping peacefully' on a locker of the abandoned ship – 'Macavity' again! – while 'the brig's boats – two – stood firm in their chocks on the roof of the deckhouse'. The writer, Kaye, acknowledged the variety of 'solutions' to the *Mary Celeste* mystery previously proposed:

> Altogether a very pretty mystery of the sea! Various 'solutions' have from time to time been published, which added imaginary details, but these may be safely disregarded. Were these all the known facts the 'mystery' would outlast mankind itself.

Fortunately, Kaye revealed, there was (yet another) *Mary Celeste* survivor to put things right: John Pemberton, the 'cook of the mystery ship', who was 'now 77 years of age' and whose memory of the 1872 incident was still 'unimpaired'. Pemberton himself does not speak directly to the reader, unlike 'Trigg' in Capt. Lucy's or 'Specioti' in Capt. Lukhmanoff's stories. Kaye is the storyteller here, based on his man Pemberton's 'unimpaired' memory of events.

He first offered a brief summary of the '*Marie Celeste*'. Some of the details were correct. One which was not concerned how she came to be named, including that her owner in 1867, Mr J.H. Winchester, 'chartered her to a New York company – Bremmer Brothers' and she 'was then renamed Mary Sellars':

> When Mr. Pemberton joined her she was trading between Philadelphia and Brazil. The name *Mary Sellars* was spoken by the Latins of Brazil as *Marie Celeste*, which name was at last painted on the stern; but *Marie* occasionally became *Mary* in the repainting.

That might have been the first but would not be the last heard about the morph from '*Mary Sellars*' to *Marie* or *Mary Celeste*. The details Kaye presented about the ship's 1872 voyage included that she loaded 'railway timber, and whale oil in barrels'. The rest of the account was likewise fictitious, apart from the fact that the vessel was bound for Genoa and intercepted by the *Dei Gratia*, though by means that in no way remotely resembled the actual events.

The germ of the incident was that there was too much whale oil for the '*Marie Celeste*' to carry. Her owners part-chartered the *Dei Gratia* to carry the surplus. Capt. Briggs – he got that name right – had no crew, because 'none of these men would sail with oil, which on a hot day afloat is martyrdom to the senses', meaning it stank like Billy-O. Capt. 'Moorhouse' had fourteen crew on his *Dei Gratia* 'of 765 tons burthen', so he loaned three men to Capt. Briggs. Three others were found by the 'boarding-master' to make up a sufficient crew for the '*Marie Celeste*'.

Dei Gratia would first go to Queenstown, Ireland, 'with a consignment of wines'. It would then proceed to 'Santa Marta in the Azores, there to meet *Marie Celeste* on arrival' and where Capt. Briggs would engage three sailors and return the three *Dei Gratia* men to their own ship.

Kaye wrote that the '*Marie Celeste*' sailed from New York 'on October 7', in 1872 – a month before she actually sailed – with '10 souls' on board. All ten, apart from the captain and his wife (no mention of a young daughter), were figments of Pemberton's/Kaye's imagination:

Mr Hullock, a hard-core American mate 'synonymous with slave-driver'; Jack Dossell, boatswain and carpenter; Tom Moffat, Charlie Manning and Billie Hawley, able seamen on loan from the *Dei Gratia*; Peter Sanson and Carl Venboldt ('a farm hand from Ohio who had come to New York without intention of leaving dry land' but was 'shanghaied' into the crew), American ordinary seamen; and cook John Pemberton, 'British-born'.

Four days before sailing: 'On October 3 a piano was hoisted aboard, and Captain Briggs's wife joined the ship.' That instrument of pleasure – the melodeon of the real *Mary Celeste* – was to become the instrument of havoc central to Pemberton's 'true story of the brig *Marie Celeste*' to explain 'the mystery which has hung round her name'.

The 'piano' put the hard-bitten mate Hullock 'in an evil mood' at the start of the voyage:

> He had been ousted from his berth in the cabin by Mrs. Briggs and her piano, which had been lashed thwartships [width-ways across the ship] against the cabin bulkhead, where the mate had designed to stow his sea-chest.

When, at the beginning of November, the 'piano' shook loose from rough weather, Hullock re-secured it in a 'fore and aft' position, which 'simple action proved to be the genesis of what has ever since been known as the classic mystery of the sea'.

All hell broke loose, and with it Mrs Briggs' 'piano', on 24 November, when they were 'roughly 400 miles north-west of the Azores, and expecting to fall in with *Dei Gratia* at any moment'. A sudden squall put the ship on her side. Mrs Briggs was at her 'piano' at the time. It got 'torn from its lashings and crashed forward upon [her], jamming her against the opposite bulkhead', and she 'was mortally stricken'. Death by piano.

The distraught Capt. Briggs, 'clearly out of his mind' by his wife's demise, accused the bully mate Hullock of 'contriving the fatality' out of spite for Mrs Briggs' piano taking the space he wanted for his sea-chest, and that he had stowed it in a fore-and-aft position 'so that it should feel the weather' and break loose. A few days later 'Captain Briggs ordered Peter Sanson to be thrown overboard'. When the crew refused, he ordered the piano to be deep-sixed, which it was since 'no one could bear the sight of the instrument'.

That same night Capt. Briggs disappeared; 'gone after the piano,' said mate Hullock. Kaye was less circumspect: 'Lest there be misconceptions, let it be stated Mr. Pemberton is convinced that Captain Briggs jumped into the sea.' On 29 November, Carl Venboldt and Hullock were both 'inflamed with the liquor which was being freely issued from the cabin store' when Venboldt accused the mate of murdering Mrs Briggs. 'Following a scuffle, he [Venboldt] was accidentally pushed into the sea' and 'astonishing as it seems no attempt was made at rescue'.

Just off the shore of 'Santa Marta' Hullock, Jack Dossell and Peter Sanson 'wasted no time in clearing off the brig' and deserted by going ashore in one of the local 'bum-boats' surrounding her. Cook Pemberton and the three *Dei Gratia* men, Tom Moffat, Charlie Manning and Billie Hawley, stayed behind to await the arrival of the *Dei Gratia*, as agreed before the two ships sailed.

They waited until 4 December. With no sign of the *Dei Gratia*, they decided to 'cruise along towards Gibraltar in the hope of intercepting the incoming vessel'. This they did 'on the morning of December 7 at 10 o'clock' when '*Dei Gratia* was sighted bowling along from north-west'.

That, said Kaye/Pemberton, was how the 'finding' of the *Mary Celeste* occurred: with three *Dei Gratia* men already aboard her, 'reinforced by a mate and one ordinary seaman' transferred from the *Dei Gratia* to sail her into Gibraltar as a salvage prize.

And, of course, with 'cook John Pemberton' on board as well, who would later recount 'the true story of the brig *Marie Celeste*, and an exact and complete explanation of the "mystery" associated with her'.

Well, that was Lee Kaye's story, at least. Except that there was no 'Lee Kaye', as such. His identity was later revealed to be a man named Laurence J. Keating, who used the initials of his first and last names as a pseudonym for his mythical 'John Pemberton' account.

It was the first of three stories penned by Keating that constituted an infamous trilogy of John Pemberton fictions about the *Mary Celeste* mystery. The last, his book *The Great Mary Celeste Hoax: A Famous Sea Mystery Exposed*, was published in 1929. It was, astonishingly, accepted quite widely as a plausible – some even said most probable – solution of The Greatest Sea Mystery. But, as they say on some news programmes, more on that later.

The second in the trilogy appeared as an article in a London newspaper, the *Evening Standard*, on 6 May 1929. It was headlined 'The Last Survivor Of The *Mary Celeste* tells A Tale That Joseph Conrad Might Have Written' and was essentially the same story told by 'Lee Kaye' three years before. This time, though, it was 'From Our Special Correspondent – Liverpool', who was, pseudonymously and anonymously, none other than Keating – again.

Monday, May 6, 1929. THE EVENING STANDARD.

THE LAST SURVIVOR OF THE *Mary Celeste* *tells* A TALE THAT JOSEPH CONRAD MIGHT HAVE WRITTEN.

On December 7, 1872, at ten o'clock in the morning, a ship was sighted in the Atlantic, sailing with a full spread of canvas towards the Spanish coast. As she did not respond to signals and showed no signs of life when viewed through the glasses, the skipper of the hailing vessel sent a boat's crew to investigate. The stranger was the brig Mary Celeste. In the forecastle were five seamen's chests and two canvas kit-bags, still containing the outfits of the crew. The galley-range, though raked out, was still hot. A cat was peacefully asleep on a locker. A meal was laid on a table in the after-cabin. Three cups of tea were lukewarm. The vessel had been abandoned precipitately for no apparent reason. It was the world's greatest mystery of the sea.

From Our Special Correspondent.
LIVERPOOL, Monday.

"AY, 'twas a music-box, a pianny, that played the biggest part in the mystery of the Mary Celeste. A cottage pianny that they used to call in the American free-and-easies a 'parlour Poll.'

... does not mind if you regard him as at times a little irascible. That is his privilege.

Always he wears an old-fashioned tailcoat. It is the habit of a lifetime. Some of his friends say the tailcoat is that in which he came to Liverpool 57 years ago, direct from the drama of the Mary Celeste. He celebrated that occasion by "having his photey took," probably for the only time in his life.

Two Overcoats Warmer.

His individuality reveals itself in typical phrases. You tell him it is warm. "Yes, two overcoats warmer than yesterday." "This piano of which you speak. Was it heavy?" "No, not heavy, massive." "And the shape of it?" "Just like a box of bacon."

This last simile is understandable.

"I was the cook in the Mary Celeste," he explained. "As a boy in Liverpool, where my father was a well-known character known as 'the crossing-sweeper of Bold-street,' I knew often enough what it was to go hungry, and I determined to be a cook, to be always near where the food is. And all my life I've been a cook.

"Not, mind you, like some of these people who call themselves cooks to-day, but a real cook.

"True, the mate of the Mary Celeste—I called him 'Starlight' Hullock because of his red nose—used to refer to me as 'Young poison,' but that is a common enough reference at sea to a cook, who is supposed to kill the people he doesn't like. I didn't mind that from him, but it was a different thing altogether when I ...

... ill-luck. If it hadn't been with us there would never have been a Mary Celeste mystery. It caused bad language the moment it came aboard. It was so awkward to handle and it was so like a woman to bring it. Mrs. Briggs, the wife of the captain, of course, was responsible. She wouldn't sail without it.

"They put it in a bit of a recess in the cabin between the port and starboard bulkheads, and Starlight Hullock was furious. He said he had no leg room and that the playing of it interfered with sleep.

"Hullock was a great powerful man from Baltimore, with hands like block of mahogany.

"'I wouldn't care,' he said to me, 'if she had brought a concertina or a fiddle, but to bring a big pianny aboard without so much as a "by-your-leave" is too much. Every time I turn in to sleep she plays her fandango, and I'm not going to stand it. She does it deliberately.'

Hurricane and Hymns.

"The relief from the trouble, or some of it, came in an unexpected way. Four days out from New York there was a terrible storm, and the pianny broke loose from its lashings. It was starting to break up the cabin as it was flung this way and that, when the mate went in. Big as it was he picked it up, and lashed it in a new position.

"Mrs. Briggs was mad. She ordered the carpenter to move it back to the old place, but the mate told the carpenter to leave it alone, and the captain couldn't interfere with a man like the mate.

"I didn't realise until afterwards that behind where the pianny was lashed before was a store of liquor that the mate wanted.

* * * *

"Well, the mate got more leg room, and more sleep, and we were having a spell of fine weather when November 24, 1872, came along. That was the day on which the last entry was made by the captain in the log of the Mary Celeste. The vessel was picked up, you remember, ten days later without a soul on board, and yet in perfect order, and no one ever found a trace of the crew.

The original *Evening Standard* article of the 'John Pemberton' story. (*Evening Standard*, 6 May 1929)

The 'Tale That Joseph Conrad Might Have Written' began with a brief summary of the *Mary Celeste* incident. It reprised some 'Lee Kaye' features and other more common myths, though, almost astonishingly, the 'Special Correspondent' from Liverpool got her name right throughout:

> On December 7, 1872, at ten o'clock in the morning, a ship was sighted in the Atlantic, sailing with a full spread of canvas towards the Spanish coast. As she did not respond to signals and showed no signs of life when viewed through the glasses, the skipper of the hailing vessel sent a boat's crew to investigate. The stranger was the brig *Mary Celeste*.
>
> In the forecastle were five seamen's chests and two canvas kit-bags, still containing the outfits of the crew. The galley-range, though raked out, was still hot. A cat was peacefully asleep on a locker. A meal was laid on a table in the after-cabin. Three cups of tea were lukewarm. The vessel had been abandoned precipitately for no apparent reason. It was the world's greatest mystery of the sea.

Most of the article comprised the narrative by the fictional cook John Pemberton, as directly spoken to the reader and transcribed by 'Special Correspondent' Keating, repeating the essence of Lee Kaye's story from three years before. Only John Pemberton, apparently '77 years of age' in 1926, put on some pretty rapid ageing, as he appeared now 'aged 92, at leisure in his little home on the outskirts of Liverpool'. The whole article was really an advertisement for Keating's recently published book, as 'Special Correspondent' Keating introduced the miraculously nonagenarianised cook:

> He is the sole survivor of the brigantine *Mary Celeste*, and he is mentioned in the book, 'The Great Mary Celeste Hoax,' by Mr. Laurence Keating, just published, in which the mystery is cleared up once and for all.

This newspaper piece is much more entertaining than the Keating alter ego Lee Kaye's of 1926. It doesn't matter that Pemberton's character is almost certainly fictional. He hits the reader directly between the eyes with his folksily contrived language right from the opening paragraphs:

> 'Ay, 'twas a music-box, a pianny, that played the biggest part in the mystery of the *Mary Celeste*. A cottage pianny that they used to call in the American free-and-easies a "parlour Poll". But none of us ever dreamt for a moment when we saw that pianny shipped to please the captain's wife that it was to bulk so large in the world's greatest mystery of the sea that I have now cleared up once and for all.'

Keating goes on to describe how Pemberton came to be the cook on the *Mary Celeste*:

> 'I was the cook in the *Mary Celeste*,' he explained. 'As a boy in Liverpool, where my father was a well-known character known as "the crossing-sweeper of Bold-street," I knew often enough what it was to go hungry, and I determined to be a cook, to be always near where the food was. And all my life I've been a cook.'

And the reason he wanted to tell his story now? Because:

> '... the mate of the *Mary Celeste* – I called him "Starlight" Hullock because of his red nose – used to refer to me as "Young poison," but that is a common enough reference at sea to a cook, who is supposed to kill the people he doesn't like.
>
> 'I didn't mind that from him, but it was a different thing altogether when I saw in an American magazine a few years ago that the real clue to the mystery of the *Mary Celeste* was that the cook – meaning me – poisoned everybody on board, threw the bodies overboard and then fell in after them.

> 'That annoyed me so much I decided to break the silence I kept for fifty years. I insisted on my friend Mr. Keating making this book. It is my vindication. I can go to the grave satisfied with it. You will find the full story there, and if it does not give you a thrill there must be something the matter with you.'

The cook who poisoned everybody and threw the bodies overboard was the central part of the story cobbled together by Arthur Morrison's proposed solution to the *Mary Celeste* mystery in the English magazine *The Strand*, in July 1913. Except that he, Joseph Hallers, known as 'Holy Joe', was an AB, or able-bodied seaman, not a cook. A cook who did throw all his poisoned victims overboard appeared in a much earlier version of the *Mary Celeste* mystery, originally published in the *Washington Post* in 1885, a suggestion, it said, that came to the US State Department 'from a Frenchman'.

That desire for 'vindication' prodded old Pemberton to recount the same Lee Kaye story of the storm-loosed 'pianny', told this time in Pemberton's own words, which much improved the tenor and amusement of the yarn:

> 'It was so awkward to handle, and it was so like a woman to bring it. Mrs. Briggs, the wife of the captain, of course, was responsible. She wouldn't sail without it. They put it in a bit of a recess in the cabin between the port and starboard bulkheads, and Starlight Hullock was furious. He said he had no leg room and that the playing of it interrupted with sleep.
>
> 'Hullock was a great powerful man from Baltimore, with hands like blocks of mahogany. "I wouldn't care," he said to me, "if she had brought a concertina, or a fiddle, but to bring a big pianny aboard without so much as a 'by-your-leave' is too much. Every time I turn in to sleep she plays her fandango, and I'm not going to stand it. She does it deliberately."'

Hurricane and Hymns

'The relief from the trouble, or some of it, came in an unexpected way. Four days out from New York there was a terrible storm, and the pianny broke loose from its lashings. It was starting to break up the cabin as it was flung this way and that, when the mate went in. Big as it was he picked it up, and lashed it in a new position.

'Mrs. Briggs was mad. She ordered the carpenter to move it back to the old place, but the mate told the carpenter to leave it alone, and the captain couldn't interfere with a man like the mate. I didn't realise until afterwards that behind where the pianny was lashed before was a store of liquor that the mate wanted.

'Well, the mate got more leg room, and more sleep, and we were having a spell of fine weather when November 24, 1872, came along. That was the day on which the last entry was made by the captain in the log of the *Mary Celeste*. The vessel was picked up, you remember, ten days later without a soul on board, and yet in perfect order, and no one ever found a trace of the crew.

'On that Sunday morning, without the slightest warning, we hit a hurricane squall. Enormous waves swamped us, the steersman was washed away from the wheel, and we thought the ship had gone. In the midst of it there was a shriek from the cabin. The tinkling at the pianny had stopped. Mrs. Briggs had been playing hymn tunes on it.

Rum

'I went down to the cabin after a while with Captain Briggs, and the sight was terrible. The pianny had been flung across the cabin and lay bobbing up and down in the water. Mrs. Briggs had been flung with it and lay underneath. She was unconscious. I was ordered to get some hot water and rushed off. I couldn't light the fire and dare not go back. The mate said a tot of rum would be better. The mate, after seeing the ship was put right, went to bed; the captain stood beside his unconscious wife all through the night.

'At the morning watch we were told that Mrs. Briggs was dead. The captain had gone "off his head," and wouldn't leave the body of his wife. The pianny lay all upsey-downsey, and the captain was kicking at it and cursing it wildly. We were all scared. There was talk of the evil luck that Mrs. Briggs and her pianny had brought. The mate took more and more rum. The captain stayed in the cabin whimpering.

'Then the mate, who had been saying all day the body must be buried, ordered Jack Dossell, the carpenter, to prepare a shroud. The captain, who had placed the pianny back in position, was in the cabin. He would not allow the body to be taken. There was a row between him and the mate. The captain accused the mate of having murdered Mrs. Briggs by altering the position of the pianny, and said he now wanted to cover up the crime by throwing the body overboard.

Burial of the Piano

'The mate was alarmed at this new turn and came up to think how he could escape a charge that might be difficult to answer on shore. Then savagely he announced that, captain or no captain, the body was going to be buried. But when three men were sent into the cabin they returned with the news that the captain was bathing the body from a bucket of alcohol, evidently with the idea of embalming it and producing it on shore to prove Hullock's guilt.

'However, the burial took place, and then occurred something that was enough to make your hair go up and never come down again. The captain ordered that Peter Sanson, who was the steersman when the big wave came that made the pianny break away, was to be sewn up in canvas at once and thrown over the side.

'The mate struggled with the captain and they both fell down the companion way. There was a pause, and when Hullock returned he had been drinking again. He brought up bottles of rye whisky for the whole of the crew and wild scenes followed.

'Later Hullock announced he had at last persuaded Briggs that the culprit was not the steersman but the pianny, and that had to be buried instead. The pianny was at once pulled up out of the cabin and pitched overboard.

'It had brought all the ill-luck (and you will see by the book how much more followed), but looking back on it all I think it was a waste of a good pianny to chuck it overboard. I wish they had given it to me. It was a good pianny.'

Just like a box of bacon.

As a final word to preface Keating's own 'Mary Celeste Hoax' book:

> The greatest of all sea mysteries was a sham. It was concocted by Captain Moorhouse, of the brig *Dei Gratia* for the sake of the salvage money obtainable by finding a derelict ship. Captain Moorhouse's mate revealed the details about the warm cups of tea and the cat. The details were true. The tea was about to be drunk by the three men who remained in the brig after the death of Captain Briggs and his wife. Hullock and the rest had deserted at the port of Santa Marta.

Capt. 'Moorhouse's' mate, Oliver Deveau, of course revealed no such 'true' details 'about the warm cups of tea and the cat' because, of course, like 'Macavity', the mythical mystery mischief-maker, they were not there! But it was a pretty good yarn nonetheless. And old Pemberton lived on within the pages of Keating's *The Great Mary Celeste Hoax* book, which has since become an icon of the *Mary Celeste* mythosphere.

Much later, in 1972, a columnist on the *Liverpool Echo*, Derek Whale, referred to the Pemberton character in Keating's 1929 'Hoax' book with evident scepticism. His review of the book, published in the *Echo* on 4 December 1972, seemed to accept the truth of Keating's 'cat asleep on a locker', amongst other *Mary Celeste* myths ('the galley stove was still warm', 'three cups of tea stood lukewarm', and the *Dei Gratia*'s 'Moorhouse took *Mary Celeste* in tow' to Gibraltar).

But Pemberton as cook?:

> Yet in 1932, a Mr. J.C. Anakin, of Boaler Street, Liverpool, who spent a lifetime and a lot of money investigating the *Celeste* affair, claimed that he had irrefutable evidence that an American named Edward

> Head, not Pemberton, had sailed as cook. Pemberton had sailed with Briggs on other voyages, but not on that fateful one.
>
> And so the mystery continued to deepen.

Indeed.

The other mini-mystery within that mythosphere is, who *was* Laurence J. Keating? Not much is known about him. When Macdonald Hastings, the author of *Mary Celeste: A Centennial Record*, published in 1972, tried to find out, for inclusion in his book, he had a letter from 'Captain T.E. Elwell, in the Isle of Man', who remarked that Keating was 'the worst type of Liverpool Irishman'. And, as far as who Keating was, that was about it.

The Myth-Deniers

At least one person, amongst others no doubt, questioned that there ever was a *Mary Celeste* incident of a mysterious nature, and suggested that the whole thing was just a myth. A certain D.G. Ball, who appeared to have some personal connection with the seafaring community, wrote a letter to the *Nautical Gazette*, published in its July 1922 edition, outlining his quandary:

> Sir.– There are many people of the sea who have heard and read about the brig *Marie Celeste*.

Ball then summarised the background to the story. He included the real myth of a warm breakfast on the table and noted that 'this story could be at any time verified at Lloyd's, the very Bible of Shipping we all know':

> The writer [i.e., Ball] had the pleasure and honour to be taken over Lloyd's and introduced to several of the members. I remembered the story of the *Marie Celeste* and was most anxious and curious to have

> this story verified, and, sailor like, I have often repeated the story over the tea cups. It may interest others to know that I was laughed out of court and given to understand that there are no records of this story of the *Marie Celeste* at Lloyd's.
>
> They have on several occasions thrashed the matter out and come to the conclusion that the whole story is just a myth without any foundation of fact. I was really sorry to hear it, because I have really believed in the *Marie Celeste*. I ask the question, is it true? If so, where are the records and how did this most remarkable story first start?
>
> If it is a fact that there never was a Flying Dutchman, there never was a William Tell and no shooting the apple off his son's head, and no Robin Hood of bow and arrow fame, I ask now have we to give up the *Marie Celeste*? If we do, we shall have nothing left.

Now, apart from the fact that Lloyd's own daily shipping newspaper *Lloyd's List* mentioned the *Mary Celeste* four times, factually, in its Casualties section in December 1872 alone, and, moreover, printed the first '*Marie Celeste*' version of her name on 1 March 1873, correspondent Ball alluded to a rather profound point: if, in the absence of truth, we only have the mystique of myths 'without any foundation of fact' that can be disbelieved and discredited, 'we shall have nothing left'.

We do, of course, have facts, though not the ultimate truth, about the *Mary Celeste* mystery. And, notwithstanding the assertion by its members, so too did Lloyd's at the time: the 'alternative facts' of denial.

PART III

THE MYSTIQUE

'Lord! said my mother, what is all this story about?

- A Cock and a Bull, said Yorick -
And one of the best of its kind, I ever heard.'

Final words of *The Life and Opinions of Tristram Shandy, Gentleman*, published 1759–66
by Laurence Sterne (1713–68)

'Solutions'

By the end of the 1920s the *Mary Celeste* myth-makers had churned out in her wake all the myths and fake news there was ever going to be about her mysterious abandonment. There was the press of full canvas and all sails set found on the derelict; the warm food and hot galley stove; the various number of the ship's boats either gone or still on board. There was also the number of people on board, ranging from, correctly, ten to more than enough hands – over twenty – to sail a ship four times her size. The names of the captains of both the *Mary Celeste* and *Dei Gratia* varied (Briggs, Griggs, Boyce, Morehouse, Moorhouse et al.), as did those of their crews. There was the sighting of 'Macavity!'; the date of her sailing; that she sailed from Boston; that her cargo included whale oil and other things besides the only cargo she actually did carry, 1,701 barrels of alcohol. All these imagined narratives were concocted by mis-chroniclers, intentional or otherwise, as was the widespread notion from the earliest years of the *Mary Celeste* mythosphere that the ship was named the '*Marie Celeste*' – and, at one time, the '*Mary Sellars*'.

From 'Mary Sellars' to 'Marie Celeste' to Mary Celeste

The origins of the once-upon-a-time '*Mary Sellars*' name came from Keating, or rather from 'Lee Kaye', in 1926. Keating then elaborated upon it three years later under his own name in his 'Hoax' book.

An American newspaper, the *Detroit Evening News*, in its magazine section of 23 May 1943, neatly summarised the evolution of '*Mary Sellars*' to '*Marie Celeste*' to *Mary Celeste*. After the article trundled through the stories of Abel Fosdyk, Capt. Lucy and his *Mary Celeste* informant Trigg, and Laurence Keating's John Pemberton fantasy, it arrived at the '*Mary Sellars*' fable. Of that, Keating's fingerprints, from his 'Hoax' book, were all over it:

> Mysteries Of The Sea – Will They Ever Be Solved?
> … In March, 1867, Captain Winchester, owner, made the following announcement in the *New York Journal*:
>
> 'We, Messrs. Winchester, Hart and Briggs (master) as owners, propose in respect of our brig *Amazon*, 282 tons gross, 216 tons net registered, to change her name to *Mary Sellars*; the same to be registered at New York, as owned by James H. Winchester and partners.'

This 'announcement' is cribbed directly from Keating's 'Hoax' book at the start of his little vignette about how the *Amazon* name changed to *Mary Celeste* via '*Mary Sellars*':

> Remember that on the lockets found in the cabin of the abandoned vessel were marked the initials M.S. And among books and music found in the cabin was one marked: 'A present to M. Sellars from her sister Alice, Jersey City, 1869.'

Hard to remember something that didn't actually exist. But moving on:

> For Mary Sellars was the sweetheart of Captain Briggs. She married him and disappeared with him two years later. Obviously, since M. Sellars was not yet the captain's wife in 1869, it seems unlikely that she could have been the mother of a 'good sized child' in 1872.
>
> The *Mary Sellars* made many trips to Brazil carrying railroad iron to a firm of French contractors there. It is suggested that the Frenchmen grew to call the little ship *Marie Celeste* since that was easier for them to pronounce than the brig's real name. In fact that name appeared on some of her bills of lading. And for some time the brig sailed with the name *Marie Celeste* painted on her stern and *Mary Sellars* on her bows.
>
> This, being noticed by a port official at Philadelphia, had to be changed. Winchester was in favour of *Marie Celeste*. But Briggs, holding out for his sweetheart's name, had to be content with half of it. And the new name was *Mary Celeste*. Thus it appears in the Shipping Register and in the Admiralty documents at Gibraltar.

Sarah Briggs would no doubt have taken considerable exception to her husband's having had a 'sweetheart' named 'Mary Sellars', and that he even married her! Utter and complete stuff and nonsense, of course, but of a piece with Keating's fertile imagination. An Australian newspaper columnist, Edward Samuel, rightfully disdained the story:

> I have heard that yarn of her being called *Mary Sellars*, after the captain's wife, but this yarn of the Frenchman painting her name on the bows as *Marie Celeste* is beyond all believing. Just suppose that the French hand, of whom there is no mention on the crew list, had painted the name wrong, would the mate not have seen the mistake?

> The usual routine was for the mate to walk along the wharf every morning and inspect the bow and head-gear. Surely he would have noticed the change in name; and would not Capt. Briggs have seen it when walking down to his ship? And are we to suppose the name was painted wrong on both bows and the stern? This is about the silliest of the many stories about the ship.[17]

Sensible man, that Edward Samuel. He even corrected the general usage of 'brig' for the *Mary Celeste*: 'The *Mary Celeste* was a wooden brigantine (not a brig) of 282 gross tons.' Unfortunately he blotted his copy-book later on by repeating oft-quoted myths such as that the ship was found with 'all sails set', that the *Dei Gratia*'s Capt. Morehouse went on her in a second boarding, that 'the remains of a meal' were on a table in the main cabin, and that she 'was towed into Gibraltar by the *Dei Gratia*', amongst other anecdotes. Even so, his version of events was more accurate than most.

His proposed solution to the mystery of her abandonment was shared, in parts, by other solutionist sleuths of the *Mary Celeste* mystery over the years: that the crew, fearful of an explosion of gases from the cargo of alcohol, got off in a boat; that the deserted ship sailed away from them; and that, on heading for the Azorean shore 6 miles away, 'getting into a line of breakers, the boat may have capsized and all hands been drowned'.

'Solutions' to the *Mary Celeste* mystery were not lacking in number. They began to mushroom shortly after the vessel arrived in Gibraltar. Suggestions of piracy, mutiny, mayhem and murder were freely and unsubstantiatedly aired. Piracy was a favourite early on:

> Pirates On The Atlantic
>
> It is now believed that the fine brig *Mary Celeste*, of about 236 tons, commanded by Capt. Benjamin Briggs, of Marion, Mass., was seized by pirates in the latter part of November, and that, after murdering the captain, his wife, child and officers, the vessel was abandoned near the Western Islands [Azores], where the miscreants are supposed to have landed.[18]

In 1904 J.L. Hornibrook came up with the creative suggestion, you might remember, that a giant octopus had tentacled away all ten souls of the *Mary Celeste*. In that *Chambers's Journal* article, Hornibrook dismissed the possibility of a piratical attack on the *Mary Celeste*:

> Piracy may be put on one side, for piracy was as unknown in the Atlantic in the sixties [1860s] as it is at the present day.

Almost thirty years later he revised that impossibility as a distinct likelihood, in an article titled 'New Light on the *Marie Celeste* Case', in the March 1933 edition of *Chambers's Journal*. He seemed encouraged to make the case for piracy now with the support of a well-known mariner of the time, Capt. J.L. Vivian Millett, who had been an apprentice on board the famous clipper *Cutty Sark* in 1884–85.

Hornibrook set out his store for a new hypothesis:

> Briefly, it is this: In the early hours of that December morning, before it was yet full daylight, the *Marie Celeste* was swooped down upon by Riff pirates, who made captives of all on board. It is easy to scoff at the idea of piracy in the nineteenth century, but it might be well to pause and reflect before scoffing.

At which point Hornibrook riffed on about the menace of piracy still operating in the 1870s, 'ascertained' by Capt. Millett. He continued:

> It is not difficult to conjure up a picture of the scene on board [the *Mary Celeste*] at the moment. Besides the man at the wheel, there was probably only one other seaman on deck. Suddenly he caught sight of the Moorish galleys dashing down on the brig. He raised a shout, and ran for the nearest weapon, which happened to be the cutlass. (This weapon, as was ascertained at Gibraltar [no, it wasn't], was usually stowed away in a locker aft [no, it wasn't].)

> Armed with the cutlass, he made for the bows, where he may have seen the pirates in the act of clambering on board. It is not improbable that the two slashes resulted from a vain attempt to repel.

And so, Hornibrook conjectured, the pirates seized the crew and Mrs Briggs and her daughter and 'hustled [them] into the galleys lying alongside'. Tossing the hatch aside on the deck, the Riff ruffians raided the cargo. 'To their disgust' they found that 'it contained alcohol', which was 'anathema to the Moslem Moor'. So they took their captives and sailed to the coast:

> Hustled away inland, driven on relentlessly day after day, with lifelong slavery awaiting them at the end of the journey – that was their destiny. Better far had they found a grave in the depths of the Atlantic.

And, of course, that 'grave in the depths of the Atlantic' was almost certainly the actual final resting place of the ten *Mary Celeste* souls.

Filling the Vacuum of Truth

What propagated the plethora of such suppositions was the mystique of a great mystery that, then as ever to this day, cried out for a solution. No matter how irrational the reasoning of 'solutions', the *Mary Celeste* mystery was a vacuum that simply needed to be filled.

Over and over again, the myths flew up like flights of gryphons to become an integral part of the *Mary Celeste* mystique. They stoked the 'solutions' of The Greatest Sea Mystery. They satisfied the need for a kind of truth, as beliefs or convictions or contentions, to fill the vacuum of its great unknown.

An Australian quarterly journal, *The Home*, published an account of the *Mary Celeste* mystery in its April 1926 edition. It issued a challenge to readers to offer suggested solutions, with 'a prize for any theory that sounds even remotely possible'. The next edition, in June, published letters that offered two possibilities: the first, 'by Mr. Herbert A. Jones, of Brisbane', cited what he believed to be 'the true solution' from 'the November issue of the *Strand* magazine for the year 1913 (a copy of which is beside me as I write)', namely, the Abel Fosdyk yarn; and the second, 'Another Theory', came from '"Miss Madcap" (age 14) … and we award her a paint-box as promised', for Hornibrook's octopus tale that she repeated.

In the absence of the real truth, which was and could everlastingly be known only to the ten souls who disappeared from the *Mary Celeste*, the creation of tall tales, myths and beliefs, and full-on cock-and-bull stories was the natural human response – the only possible response – to the mystique of a mystery in the thrall of such truth-seekers.

They had, as *The Home* 'solutions' indicated, quite surprising durability. And quite a few of those could be parked well and truly in the cock-and-bull camp, including this hypothesis that appeared in the *Nautical Magazine* of October 1913:

> The Mystery of the *Mary Celeste*
> 'As this greatest mystery of the sea,' writes Mr. William F. Bernsten, an old Cardiff marine engineer, 'was brought into the great prominence it holds to-day through the *Nautical Magazine*, it seems to me fit and proper to send a solution which has occurred to me to that journal.'

A mumber of facts about the mystery ship were known, according to engineer Bernsten: that 'the mate of the *Marie Celeste* never wrote up his log after the day the vessel left New York', which was not true; that 'the vessel was abandoned in calm weather', which was *probably* not true, and 'in a perfectly seaworthy condition', which *was* true; and that 'the chronometer and ship's papers were missing', true, but that 'this is all we really know', not true.

Bernsten's erroneous assumption that 'there must have been some reason for the mate of the *Marie Celeste* forgetting one of his principal duties – the log-book', suggested, he contended, 'that the mate of that vessel became desperately in love with the captain's wife and that, at all hazards, he was determined to gain his prize'.

The imaginative Cardiff theorist then hypothesised that 'a foreign sailing craft' appeared near the *Mary Celeste*, and 'may have been flying distress signals'. This would have caused the master of the *Mary Celeste* to have 'sent his mate aboard to make inquiries', as the 'natural and seamanlike' thing to do.

Suppose further, he conjectured, that the mate 'was informed that the master was dead, that they were short-handed, wanted a navigator, and that their chronometer had been ruined in bad weather'. Well! Imagine that, indeed:

> 'When the mate of the *Marie Celeste* found out the stranger's plight he saw a clear road to obtain the woman he loved! "Satan works on sea and land."'

The time was ripe for – A Cunning Plan!

Berntsen mused:

> 'Could he not have sent the boat of the *Marie Celeste* back with an intimation that the captain of the distressed stranger wanted an interview and should also be pleased to see his wife and child? Remember the weather was very fine. Although it is against the unwritten law of the sea for a captain to leave his ship, there is more than a possibility that he did so, and, to give his position due honour, was rowed by four men. *This left only five on his own vessel.*
>
> 'When the visitors arrived on board they were welcomed and taken into the cabin, where the captain of the *Celeste* was seized and bound. Meanwhile his four boat hands suffered a similar fate.
>
> 'What could be easier, then, than for the erring mate to have loosened a boat belonging to the foreigner and taken the *Marie Celeste*'s boat back, hoisted it in its place, seized the chronometer and ship's papers, terrorised the rest of the crew, and rowed them back to the foreigner without leaving a trace behind?
>
> 'It may be reasonably asked, "What became of the foreigner?" My answer is, that the same question may be well asked to-day, concerning steamers and sailing vessels that leave port never to be heard of again, and that the vessel which took off the crew of the *Marie Celeste* foundered with all hands.'

The Welsh engineer's fantasy included the small matter of the *Mary Celeste*'s boat being found on board the abandoned ship after it had been 'hoisted ... in its place' by 'the erring mate' of 'the foreigner'. Of course, it wasn't – and, like the rest of the fantasy, this was the invention of a man with time on his hands to fantasise.

Capt. T.E. Elwell: *'A Chronometer Clue'*

Chambers's Journal published various *Mary Celeste* stories over the years, starting with Hornibrook's giant octopus theory in October 1904. Its July 1923 edition included an article, 'A Chronometer Clue: The *Marie Celeste* Mystery', by T.E. Elwell, who had been a master in the merchant marine and, as Macdonald Hastings wrote in his 1972 centennial book, had some personal knowledge of Laurence Keating. Capt. Elwell focused on the chronometer missing from the *Mary Celeste* when the *Dei Gratia* found her as the key clue to her mysterious abandonment. After reviewing the various accounts of the mystery in the news press and magazines of past years, Capt. Elwell began his own foray into it, poking holes into the supposed 'unanimity' of agreement about an assumed number of crew, amongst other fallacies, that was wholly mythical:

> There is a curious unanimity about the number of her crew; all accounts agree on 17 men, exclusive of the captain, his wife, and infant daughter. Here again is an item that joggles in the eyes and ears of a sailor like a billiard-ball across the mouth of a pocket. It will not go down without further help. Seventeen men is an enormous crew for a brigantine; a four-masted barque of 2,200 tons register, able to take four *Marie Celeste*s in her hold, could sail round the world with a crew of 20 men. Also, we note that three men took the brigantine into Gibraltar. This crew of piratical dimensions needs verification.

Capt. Elwell's preview included well-worn myths such as 'the galley fire was still alight', 'a meal in fresh condition was spread upon the cabin table', and 'none of her boats was missing'. Ploughing on, he proposed to 'reconstruct what happened on the high seas, a little to the south-west of the Azores, on the 24th November, 1872', the last day the ship's log was written up and ten days before the *Mary Celeste* 'apparently was abandoned on the 5th of December':

> The officer on watch [of the *Mary Celeste*] sighted an abandoned vessel, probably a steamer. He called the captain, and all hands were soon on deck, turning their eyes first toward the derelict, and then on the captain. Here was the chance that all sailors talk of, and so few see materialise. A short run into Gibraltar, and then a huge sum to be divided among them. Would the Old Man chance it?
>
> The Old Man would. The mate with two men could take the *Marie* into Gibraltar, and there wait. The major portion of the crew, himself included, would follow with the prize. There was no need to lower a boat; the brigantine could be laid alongside. Or, if a boat was lowered, the mate, with his crew of two, could make shift to hoist it again.

The stratagem, then, was for the mate and two men to stay with the *Mary Celeste* and sail her to Gibraltar. All the others would go on to the derelict steamer, take her into Gibraltar and there be rewarded with 'a huge sum' of salvage reward. 'Thus the transfer was made, the last to leave being the captain with his wife and daughter, the ship's chronometer and all papers.' And with that, and 'a ringing cheer' from the steamer men, the two vessels parted company:

> But it proved a fatal exchange. The steamer was strained; the crew proved too small for the task, and during a gale the water gained upon them. The prize was one of the cogged dice thrown by Fate at men's feet. They picked it up, made a bold throw – and lost.

The 'brigantine', meanwhile, 'is making steady progress' towards Gibraltar. And no doubt, Capt. Elwell maintained, she would have arrived safely – 'but for her cargo of alcohol'. With the imagination of his seer's eye:

> I see the mate standing his trick at the wheel, oblivious of the stealthy removal of the fore hatches under cover of the forward house. I see a barrel broached, two men filling a couple of buckets, and replacing the hatches and tarpaulin. They begin to drink, grow quarrelsome, and are soon at each other's throats.
>
> Then comes a cry of horror, for one has loosened his grip, and his victim sinks lifeless to the deck. The mate releases the wheel and rushes forward, to be met with a blow on the head with a belaying pin. As well then as afterwards, for he could never have taken the brigantine to port, handicapped as he was by a doomed man who sought his life.
>
> So two bodies are tumbled over the side, and the murderer turns again to the bucket. He exults, sings, raves, fights imaginary enemies, and while crouching on the topgallant bulwarks, shaking his fists at the screaming gulls, he leans too far, slips, and is the last of the *Marie Celeste*'s crew to die.
>
> Such may well be the solution of this classic mystery of the sea, drawn from a missing chronometer and a cargo of alcohol.

Capt. Elwell took an incontrovertible fact about the *Mary Celeste* mystery – the missing chronometer – from which he spun a hypothesis that, he suggested, might have solved the mystery. Well, it was certainly a hypothesis. It was more compatible, though, with the corps of other myth-makers' 'solutions' than with the body of documented facts about the mystery.

The Burning Ship Theory

In his 1927 book *In the Wake of the Wind Ships*, the Scots-Canadian, Montreal-domiciled writer William Frederick Wallace wrote about the *Mary Celeste*'s origins, her 1872 mystery voyage, and her life thereafter. In the book he summarised his theory about a possible reason for her mysterious abandonment from an earlier interview he gave to the *Montreal Star* published on 25 February 1925. 'Matters that appear mystifying to landsmen,' he said, 'are usually commonplace and probable to a sailor', including mysteries of the sea caused by the many perils of the sea. The *Mary Celeste* was one such mystery for which he imagined a decidedly creative solution, as he related originally to the *Montreal Star* interviewer in 1925:

> 'I must point out that the *Mary Celeste*'s people evidently left her in a very great hurry – in a panicky haste, I should assume – and left her in some other vessel's boat or boats. I cannot imagine them jumping overboard in a body. If they were threatened by some mysterious sea-creature – as has been suggested – they wouldn't leap into the sea. They'd run below. That's the most natural thing to do.'

So much for Hornibrook's writhing giant killer octopus. Wallace then dismissed other fabulisms:

> 'There was nothing in the *Mary*'s cargo to cause abandonment; there was no evidence of a madman running amok aboard of her and driving her company overboard; there was no sign of a wholesale and

sudden decimation by fever or some sudden disease, nor any sign of their being forced to leave abruptly by piratical attack.

'Undoubtedly the menace which caused abandonment came from without the ship, and it came suddenly, and without warning.'

So, Mr Wallace, what *might* that menace have been?

'If I were writing that story I might put it this way. The *Mary Celeste* was becalmed in company with another sailing ship. I would say that the other craft was loaded with coal and dynamite. I have heard of such a combination of cargo, so it's quite logical. As vessels often do when becalmed, they draw together. I can imagine the other craft drifting close to the *Mary Celeste* – possibly within a hundred feet or so. It has often happened thus.

'Then of a sudden, the crew of the stranger find their coal cargo afire – spontaneous combustion – common enough with certain coal cargoes. With the fire in close proximity to the dynamite, the crew become panic-stricken and swing out a boat – possibly the smallest and lightest boat in their haste, and in this they leave the burning ship.

'They pull over to the *Mary Celeste* and inform them of the imminent danger. A slight puff of wind may have sprung up in the meantime and caused the burning ship to draw nearer the *Celeste*. A panic naturally follows aboard the brigantine.'

The master of the burning ship then takes the *Mary Celeste* people into their small boat. And then?

'We now have a situation where the crews of two vessels have piled into a small boat. They hastily pull away from the impending calamity. There is a case of frantic oar-pulling in a crowded boat. Anything might happen then. The boat might capsize and cast all its occupants into the water. It might have been an old leaky craft which filled when its upper strakes [planks] were depressed with the unusual weight of its human freight. No baling can be done when there is no

> room to move. A catastrophe in such a case is perfectly logical, and it would be possible for every soul to drown.'
>
> 'But some could surely cling to the boat,' it was suggested. 'It wouldn't sink.'
>
> 'Yes, that's possible,' returned Mr. Wallace, 'but there are sharks in those latitudes. They'd be around in scores. They are often attracted to becalmed ships by the garbage thrown overboard.'
>
> 'But how will you get clear of the burning ship in the vicinity of the *Mary Celeste*? If she had exploded or crashed into the brigantine, there would have been traces of such a happening.'
>
> 'Undoubtedly. But perfectly logical theory will dispose of that eventuality. The burning ship, or the *Mary Celeste* for that matter, may have caught a slant of wind which drew them apart again. The *Mary* might have drifted out of danger by the time the other craft blew up. There is the possibility that she didn't blow up after all – the fire working away from the explosive and burning out the side of the ship until she capsized. Fanned along with puffs of wind, and in the grip of a current, the *Mary Celeste* might drift a considerable distance from the scene of the catastrophe.'

Well, it was certainly 'a theory'. It did, however, beg the question of why the *Mary Celeste* people might have 'piled into a small boat' from the burning ship, with catastrophic consequences, rather than get off, hurriedly, yes, but more safely, in their own boat, the one missing when the *Dei Gratia* found her. Still, the mystery and mystique of the *Mary Celeste* did beg many more questions than were ever satisfactorily answered. Mr Wallace himself was in a crowded boatload of such belief-beggars.

The Mystic's Version – or Vision – or … Something

The candidate for the most bizarre, indeed, byzantine *Mary Celeste* 'solution', such as anyone could understand it, was an unknown source in 1929 who had far too much time on their hands composing a sort of algebraic-Satanic interpretation of conjured-up mystical phenomena relating to the mystery that puzzled as much as the mystery itself. A columnist on the *Daily Herald*, a London socialist newspaper that was the predecessor of *The Sun* tabloid newspaper, 'Gadfly', took a swipe at it with mordant wit in a column titled 'Another Mystery Solved' in the edition of 12 June 1929. 'Gadfly' started off with a few well-worn myths, including the conversion of the *Mary Celeste*'s cargo into a more sailorly quaff:

> It is nearly 60 years since *Marie Celeste* was picked up somewhere off the coast of Portugal with all sails set. The brigantine, which had cleared from New York with a cargo of rum, and a personnel of 13 (including the skipper's wife, their little girl, and a couple of pier-head jumpers), was found to be deserted. Everything else was intact, barring the ship's papers and the chronometer, which were missing …

No solution, the writer observed, had ever resolved the mystery – until:

> An unknown pamphleteer … is ready to tell us all about it. It is headed '*Marie Celeste* Facts', and it appears to have some connection with the Great Pyramid. You'd be surprised, laddie!
>
> Take the dimensions of the ship for example. Listen to the anonymous hierophant [a teacher or priest who explains religious mysteries] and for bear to yelp.

There followed a mathematical equation the anonymous pamphleteer headed '*Load draught displacement for ship with *7 block co efficient of fineness =* '.

Take the dimensions of the ship, for example. Listen to the anonymous hierophant and forbear to yelp.

Load draught d:s lacement for ship with ·7 block co efficient of fineness =

98.[illegible]'x25'4'x11.24' draught / 35 cub. ft. s a water per ton x 7 = 628.32 tons or 314.16x2.

You see it all now, I hope! But that isn't the end of the shocking affair.

The mystic's 'solution': detail. (*Daily Herald*, 12 June 1929, by 'Gadfly')

As if that cleared things up, 'Gadfly' lodged tongue in cheek and remarked:

> You see it all now, I hope! But that isn't the end of the shocking affair. 'Cleared from Hell Gate, New York, 7th November, 1872, A.D., for Genoa or Genea (not Genesis) 6.66 degrees east of Paris 0 degrees, with 1,700 barrels of SPIRITS, each barrel containing 31½ or 31.416 gallons.' That makes it much easier, I hope. And thirstier.

But our unknown friend doesn't leave us to puzzle it out, like a lot of boneheads. He simply wades in with information tending to throw a light on this dark mystery. For instance, we are told that 'Bath [Bath, Maine, where *Mary Celeste* was sometimes said to have been built] is 3.1416 degrees north of Hell Gate and 3141.6 statute miles radius from London, Greenwich 0 degrees, and 216 miles (6x6x6) east of Hell Gate.'

Possibly the skipper of *Marie Celeste* discovered this when he sighted the Azores and gave the order 'Abandon ship' without any more ado. I don't blame him. But that is by no means the worst of the tale, believe me. For instance, it has at last leaked out that the presence of a deckhand named Goodschad had something to do with it. We are not told just what; but we are assured that Gottlieb Goodschad means 'God loves a good sheath or body.' And I should be the last to dispute it.

Moreover, it should be borne in mind that the port to which *Marie Celeste* was consigned, 'Genoa or Genes, is 914.5 miles radius from the Rock [i.e., Gibraltar], and 914.5 miles is the circumference of a circle whose area is 66,600. *Lusitania* sunk 914.5 miles west of Berlin in 41.613 fathoms.'

(The *Lusitania* was actually sunk off the south coast of Ireland by a German U-boat on 7 May 1915 in just over 50 fathoms of water.)

I don't think there is any gainsaying that, though the captain of the Lucie might have been told about it at the time. Anyhow, to sum it all up, our unknown guide and mystery solver concludes in this fashion:

'A goodly pi-ship made under the auspices of The Trinity, christened the *Marie Celeste* or Celestial Mary, was loaded up with good SPIRITS in Hell Gate in the West, and consigned to a rotten port in the east and sailed with an unholy number of crew [i.e., 13], whose mate was Bilson or Baalson [*Baal*: a false god, heathen; also, *Baal-zebud*, or *Beelzebub*]. Between St. Michael and St. Marie in Lusitanian [i.e., Portuguese] territory, the Bridegroom came for

> His Bride and spirited off the unholy number with what they stood in along with the old sailing [?] and old time measure, and gave the Bride her marriage lines and sailed her without any crew safely for many days, although she was heading for Setu-Baal in Lusitania [Setubal in Portugal] ...
>
> 'The new Prayer Book was sunk by the "Protestant underworld" and the "Celtic fringe." Although 666 votes were cast in its favours. The New Captain is THE ROCK; the new crew the Brit-Ish race; the new papers the New Testament; and the new time measure the year 1 A.D.
>
> 'Now you know. WHY NOT TELL THE OTHERS?'
>
> The description of Genoa as 'a rotten port' might please Mussolini, but – why not tell the others, for all that? Why not, indeed! True, you run the risk of getting yourself certified, but Pioneers, O pioneers! As Walt Whitman remarked. Anyway, if anybody asks you, in future, whether you can explain the mystery *Marie Celeste*, don't write to me and say, in Lloyd Georgian accents, 'Why wasn't I told?'

In *A Great Sea Mystery*, his first book about the *Mary Celeste*, in 1927, J.G. Lockhart swatted away the mystic's mumbo-jumbo with contemptuous disdain, referring to an article published in the *British Journal of Astrology* in September 1926 which was probably the same as Gadfly's mystic 'pamphleteer':

> The article is really only of interest as illustrating the nonsense which people with bees in their bonnets will solemnly set down in writing for other people with bees in their bonnets as solemnly to read.

The Brains Trustee 'Solves' the Mystery

In 1941 the BBC launched an 'informational radio discussion programme' called *The Brains Trust*. It later went on television and was hugely popular until it expired in 1961. One of its original broadcasting team of three was an ex-Royal Navy man, Commander Archibald Bruce Campbell. In a London newspaper, the *Sunday Dispatch*, on 19 April 1942, Campbell claimed, 'I Solve the Mystery of the *Marie Celeste*'.

Curiously, the author ran with the old cod-piece of a fiction about how the *Amazon* went to '*Mary Sellars*' and then *Mary Celeste* and never was '*Marie Celeste*', even though that was what she was named in the heading of the article. Still, as the saying goes: stranger things happen at sea – as Commander Campbell's 'solution' proved:

> When she was built she was named the *Amazon*. When Briggs, her captain, became part-owner he changed her name to the maiden name of his dear wife, Mary Sellars. She was being repainted by an illiterate Frenchman and the nearest he could get to 'Sellars' was 'Celeste.' She never was called 'Marie.' I saw a discharge paper, dated 1874, the other day, and on it she was spelled '*Mary Celeste*.'

Campbell then got into the meat and potatoes of his 'solution':

> When I first went to sea we had with us an old bos'n named Pike. He was then about 60 years of age. One night we were lying alongside the wharf at Wooloomooloo, Sydney Harbour. Some of us were

yarning on the fo'c'sle head when a youngster mentioned the case of the *Mary Celeste*. He related the legend as he had heard it. Pike listened intently and, when the man had finished he looked him in the face and said:

> 'As a sailor, do you really believe all that junk?'
> 'Well,' answered the man, 'it's one solution, isn't it?
> 'Not the right one by a long chalk.'
> I butted in, 'What do you know about it then, Pike?'
> This is the story he told us ...

Pike's story was that he had once shipped with 'a cook named Pemberton', who told him, 'I was the cook of the *Mary Sellars.*' Campbell's *Mary Celeste* mystery 'solution' was essentially a rehashed version of the Lee Kaye/Laurence Keating story that John Pemberton recited about the death of Mrs Briggs crushed by her run-amok piano, the derangement and suicidal leap overboard of Capt. Briggs, the conspiracy of the crew, and so on.

And so, too, not only *not* a solution but really just a recycled narrative of the Pemberton yarn the Brains Trust man had read, remembered and now affirmed:

> I honestly believe this to be the true solution of the mystery.

A Sandbank-Stranded Solution

The famous ex-whaling island of Nantucket's daily newspaper, the *Inquirer and Mirror* (still going today), of 10 September 1949 published what the newspaper's anonymous columnist remarked about the *Mary Celeste* mystery was 'a solution which at last makes sense. It was told only the other day by a former intelligence officer with whom we were lunching and was based on his own personal experience while on duty during the last World War.'

The 'former intelligence officer' was William Crosby Bennett, 78 years old at the time of his lunch date with his *Inquirer and Mirror* interlocutor. Bennett was born in Nantucket two years before the *Mary Celeste* mystery voyage, in 1870. He was latterly resident in southern California and so probably on a visit to his birthplace in the summer of 1949. Bennett's proposed solution was based on an incident he knew about 'during the closing days of World War Two when a small naval craft on a secret mission was heading south along the West African coast to contact an intelligence officer at Dakar', about 1,000 miles to the south:

> To avoid detection by enemy vessels the passage was made after dark through the uncharted and treacherous waters of the Arguin Banks, between 60 and 70 miles off shore.

The Arguin Banks are sandbanks off the northern coast of Mauretania and are numerous thereabouts. Late one night, the 'small naval craft' struck and went aground on one. The 'sand islands' were apparently well known to arise and disappear 'mysteriously' with some regularity. The commander of the craft decided to wait and see if their sandy entrapment might similarly be disengaged. After a few days they woke to 'the joyous sensation of a rocking motion', in open water, as the island sandbank 'had simply vanished'.

Bennett asked, rhetorically:

> Is it not within reason to believe that upon one of these sand islands the *Marie Celeste* grounded? Her last known location, when all was well on board, was off the Azores. The weather records of the group [i.e., the Azores] show that heavy winds prevailed at the time. The missing sails would indicate she was blown far off her course and could have been swept far to the south. In the dozen days elapsing between the last notation on the log slate and the date she was found ... she could have covered an astonishing mileage.

And then Mr Bennett's 'reasoning' of his 'solution':

> If the reasoning still holds good, those on the *Marie Celeste*, finding themselves a-ground in the treacherous waters of the Arguin Banks, completely lost their heads. Panic-stricken, they crowded into the lifeboat and rowed away from their ship which later was to float unharmed when the island sank. If the eleven persons who had been on board succeeded in reaching the coast, probably a lingering death from thirst or slaughter by savage tribesmen awaited them before the long trek to Port Etienne could be accomplished.

There is a gaping leaky hole in the hull of the former intelligence man's 'reasoning': how could the *Mary Celeste* be both stuck on a Mauritanian 'sand island' after she was 'swept far to the south' of her last logged position off the Azores, and, at that very same time, discovered by the *Dei Gratia* over a thousand miles north between the Azores and Portugal? If Mr Bennett was ever asked that question he

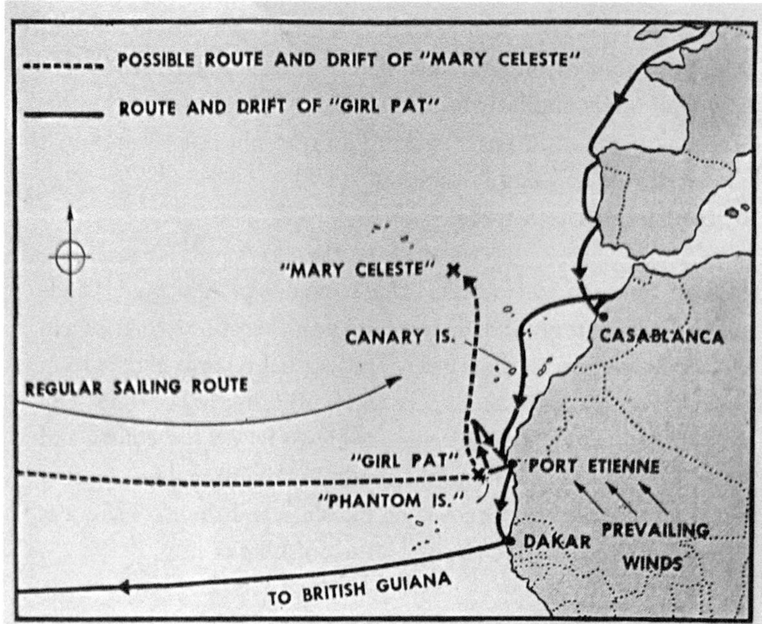

Phantom islands. (*Life*, 6 December 1948)

had precious little time to respond: he died three months later, on 21 December 1949, at his home in Los Angeles.

The doyen of *Mary Celeste* chroniclers, Charles Edey Fay, included Bennett's sand island theory in the second of two articles he wrote on the *Mary Celeste*, published in the August and September 1950 issues of *Sea Breezes* magazine. The two accounts are virtually, and suspiciously, identical, though the punctilious Fay gave more detail:

> Among the most recent attempts to explain the abandonment of the *Mary Celeste* and the disappearance of her company is that of

> Capt. Dod Orsborne, in an article titled 'The Phantom Islands' in 'Life' magazine of December 6, 1948. ['The Phantom Islands – A weird incident off Africa offers a clue to a famous mystery of the sea', by Dod Orsborne.]
>
> In 1936 he was on a job for the British Naval Intelligence [*sic* – Orsborne later *claimed*] and his diesel-powered vessel, the *Girl Pat*, 68ft. overall length, was cruising off the coast of French West Africa when she landed unexpectedly on a sandy island. After getting off, she soon landed on another, spending altogether four days thereon before getting afloat and continuing to her destination. During this time, Capt. Orsborne states, islands were rising and disappearing.

Orsborne gave exactly the same reasons as Bennett for the appearance and disappearance of the sand islands. Fay, for numerous reasons, debunked the naval captain's thought, like Bennett's, that the *Mary Celeste* might have stranded there – including the fact that indisputably 'authentic' records were 'sufficiently specific to show that the *Mary Celeste* was not 1,000 miles away' on 25 November 1872, 'somewhere off the coast of Africa – but off the coast of St. Mary's Island' in the Azores. Fay concluded with conviction:

> In view of the established facts of the case as recorded in the court testimony, I regard the 'phantom island' theory as fantastic and utterly untenable.

Dr Oliver Cobb and Charles Edey Fay

> Because of my personal knowledge of and relation to Captain Benjamin S. Briggs and his wife Sarah Everson [*sic* – Elizabeth; an editing error, apparently] (Cobb), who were cousins of mine, and my long acquaintance with their families, I feel compelled to write the story of the loss [*sic* – abandonment] of the brig *Mary Celeste* and shed some much needed light on the so-called mystery surrounding the disappearance of the captain and crew of that vessel.
>
> I desire to get before the reading public the truth so far as we know it regarding the fate of those who were on board the *Mary Celeste*, November 24th, 1872.[19]

Dr Cobb, from Easthampton, Massachusetts, researched the mystery of the *Mary Celeste* for many years, with the diligence impressed upon him by a family relationship to the Briggs. The theory he proposed as a possible solution to the mystery was cited by Charles Edey Fay, with whom he corresponded on the subject for some years, as the most likely course of events. Fay wrote, in the second of his 1950 *Sea Breezes* magazine articles on the mystery:

> Of all the theories and attempted solutions inspired by the abandonment of the vessel and the disappearance of her company, none appears so reasonable as that of the late Dr. Oliver Cobb. In his conversations and correspondence with the writer [i.e., Fay], as well as in his article in the February 1940 issue of 'Yachting', he expressed the opinion that the abandonment was due to fright caused by

> disturbing behaviour on the part of the cargo and that the main peak-halyards found 'broke and gone' afforded the correct clue as to the manner in which the abandonment was effected.
>
> My own theory agrees with this and with the belief that the weather also played an important part in the tragic happening of the forenoon of November 25, 1872.

Fay was informed about those weather conditions by a letter from the Director of the Meteorological Service in the Azores, Lieut.-Col. J. Agostinho, dated 27 May 1940. According to the only two weather stations there at the time, at Angra do Heroismo, on the island of Terceira, and Horta, on Faial, when *Mary Celeste* was sailing along the southern edge of the archipelago on the morning of 25 November 1872, 'calm or light wind' prevailed. From the mid-afternoon into the evening, however, a cold front swept across the islands, 'the wind shifting then from S.W. to N.W.'.

So during the day of 25 November *Mary Celeste* experienced 'calm or light' south-westerly breezes in the morning. These veered to strong north-westerly winds as the cold front passed over her later on. That wind-shift, Fay surmised, played an 'important part in the tragic happening of the forenoon of November 25, 1872'.

Dr Cobb, in his *Yachting* magazine article of February 1940, tried his hand at reconstructing events from the day before.

> As the entry in the log book made at noon, November 24th, indicates light southerly wind, the *Mary Celeste* was then probably under full sail. This enables us to reconstruct what probably happened.

What happened, Dr Cobb surmised, was that 'at some time after noon of November 24th' (it must actually have been on the 25th, after the last log slate entry of 8 a.m. that day), Capt. Briggs took in most of *Mary Celeste*'s sails: the big gaff mainsail on the mainmast was furled on deck; the uppermost sails on her foremast were taken in along their yards; and one of the jibs at the bow – a staysail – was doused and left lying loose on deck. That left the ship under reduced sail with two of her jibs still set, and the big foresail and upper and lower topsails set on the foremast:

> The vessel was still on the starboard tack as is shown by the jibs being set on the port side.

It was certainly far from many, if not most, *Mary Celeste* chroniclers' statements that she was 'under full sail' when found by the *Dei Gratia*.

The only reason to take in sail when winds were 'calm or light' would have been to slow the ship down. But ... why? Dr Cobb's theory:

> We do not know why, but I think that the cargo of alcohol, having been loaded in cold weather at New York early in November and the vessel having crossed the Gulf Stream and being now in comparatively warm weather, there may have been some leakage and gas may have accumulated in the hold.
>
> The captain, having care for his wife and daughter, was probably unjustifiably alarmed and, fearing a fire or an explosion, determined to take his people in the boat away from the vessel until the immediate danger should pass.

Fay essentially agreed with this theory: that alcohol loaded in cold New York might well have become somehow disturbed by passing into warmer weather around the Azores that caused some kind of leakage of alcoholic vapours:

> Captain Briggs, mindful of the nature of his cargo and the need for ventilation, decided to take advantage of the more favourable conditions then prevailing ... and ordered the removal of the fore hatch. As this was being done, there may have been an up-rush of vapour from the hold, accompanied by rumbling sounds of so alarming a nature as to create the fear on the part of the master and crew that an explosion was imminent.

Like most others before him, Dr Cobb speculated that there was 'evidence of haste in leaving the vessel'. Why? 'It may well have been that just at that time came an explosion which accounted for the fore hatch being upside down on deck, as found.' It didn't quite tally with Fay's suggestion that the fore hatch was deliberately uncovered to vent the alcoholic gases. Still, possibly for that fear of the imminent danger of an explosion destroying and sinking the ship, the *Mary Celeste* sailors launched the ship's boat, got everybody in, and took hold of the most easily accessible bit of rope, the peak halyard, to stay attached to the ship as they waited, hopefully, for the danger to pass. As Dr Cobb remarked in his *Yachting* piece:

> Whatever happened, it is evident that the boat with ten people in her left the vessel and that the peak halliard was taken as a tow line and as a means of bringing the boat back to the *Mary Celeste* in case no explosion or fire had destroyed the vessel.

But why take the peak halyard as a tow-rope when there would have been plenty of spare rope in the lazarette at the stern? The *Dei Gratia* men found the hatch cover of the lazarette taken off. This suggested that, initially, perhaps, the *Mary Celeste* men thought one of the spare coils of rope stowed there would be a good tow-rope. The peak halyard, however, fastened to a belaying-pin around the base of the mainmast, was easier to get at than a stiff and coiled rope in the lazarette. At least that was Fay's thought.

So there they were: the company of ten souls in a small boat 'not more than 16 to 20ft. long with perhaps not more than 9 to 12ins. of freeboard' – the depth of the sides of the boat above the surface of the sea – 'and a few hastily gathered necessaries including, no doubt, a small supply of food and drinking water ... trailing astern of their vessel', according to Fay. With light winds and half her sails down, *Mary Celeste* would have been idling along, with no great strain on the umbilical tow-rope attached to the boat.

Imagined parting of the boat from *Mary Celeste*. (*Yachting*, February 1940)

Then, quite suddenly, the cold front moved in. The mainly southerly or south-westerly breeze of that morning veered, in the afternoon, to westerly or north-westerly squalls that 'later became of a gale force', according to Lieut.-Col. Agostinho of the Azorean Meteorological Service. Fay noted:

> Under the impact of wind of such violence the *Mary Celeste* might have lunged forward with such suddenness as to part the towline,

> leaving the occupants of the small boat striving with frantic but futile efforts to overtake the onsweeping vessel ...
>
> It is, of course, possible that the boat, while being towed through rough waters with her bows held down by a taut towline, was swamped by the heavy seas, resulting in the drowning of all hands.

For various reasons, Fay favoured the former possibility as the more likely – the *Dei Gratia* men found the peak halyards 'broke and gone', 'carried away, gone' – but either way, 'the occupants of the boat would have been in the same perilous position'. The squally gale-force wind from the north-west 'would have blown the small boat with its company out into the broad Atlantic with about 800 miles between them and nearest mainland – the coast of Portugal ... In such circumstances the fate of the *Mary Celeste*'s company is not hard to imagine.'

Dr Cobb expressed a more blunt certainty:

> They perished – let us hope quickly.

That same wind would have driven the *Mary Celeste* herself eastwards 'out into the broad Atlantic'. She wouldn't have sailed a straight course: a loose wheel, and rudder, would have allowed her to swing about, with her five set sails fixed on starboard tack, but probably blown this way and that as she straggled along. But she would have headed generally eastwards until she met more consistent northerly winds that turned her around to head westwards – and still on starboard tack when the *Dei Gratia* found her. As mate Deveau of the *Dei Gratia* had testified at the Gibraltar Inquiry:

> I should say that from the spot marked on the chart as the last position of the *Mary Celeste* on the 24th up to the place where we found her I should say would be from five to six hundred miles. The wind was blowing from the N. to S.W. in the interval between 24th November and 5th December as near as I can tell ...

> She [*Mary Celeste*] had changed her course more than once [in that 'interval']. She was going backwards [i.e., heading west when the *Dei Gratia* found her]. It is impossible to say therefore how long or how often she had changed her course.

Charles Edey Fay expressed his final words about the *Mary Celeste*, her company of ten souls and The Greatest Sea Mystery:

> The sober, unembellished recital of the known facts concerning the vessel's experience, involving the complete disappearance of an honourable and capable shipmaster, his wife and child, and a crew of whom we find nothing except good report, needs no melodrama to make the drama interesting to the reading public. To the mature mind facts can be fascinating, and there is tragedy in the simple truth.
>
> The reason for abandonment of a seaworthy vessel and the disappearance of her company is still the greatest unsolved mystery in the annals of the sea – a mystery that seems destined to remain for ever unrevealed until the coming of that day when all whom the sea hath sundered shall be reunited and all that now lies hidden shall be made plain.

The Books: A Select Review

No one book or author encompasses the range of *Mary Celeste* accounts, records, cock-and-bull tall tales and other stories about her mystery. Each of the following, however, makes a contribution to a *Mary Celeste* literary canon that, read as a whole, ranges across a pretty broad expanse of facts, anecdotes and narratives, as well as 'fake news', 'alternative facts' and outright balderdash.

To get the most flea-bitten of all *Mary Celeste* narratives out of the way first …

Laurence J. Keating, The Great Mary Celeste Hoax: A Famous Sea Mystery Exposed (1929)

A *New York Times* reviewer of Keating's book, on 18 August 1929, soon after it was published, summarised the facts of the *Mary Celeste* mystery according to the account in Elliott O'Donnell's *Strange Sea Mysteries*, which was published 'two or three seasons ago' (1926, in fact) and was itself a morass of myth and misinformation. The reviewer opened his gambit with some prescience:

> A book around which controversy is certain to rage as soon as it is in the hands of American readers …

And concluded inconclusively:

> Whether 'The Great Mary Celeste Hoax' is ... the actual account of the brig's strange voyage, or is a yet more ingenious solution of the so-called mystery than any other so far put forth, the reader must decide for himself ... But at least the book will add to the gayety of the American nation. Let them fight it out!

Keating's 'Hoax' book is a great lumbering shaggy dog story of the extended John Pemberton yarn as the old cook of the *Mary Celeste*. For all Keating's insistence on its verity, it had more fleas on it than might infest a hundred *Mary Celeste*s. In the first few pages he asserted that:

> The purpose of the present narrative is to put on record an exact and accurate account of what really did happen on board the vessel during her famous and magical voyage, to explain why and how she was abandoned, and to reveal what became of the crew.

Keating went on to beg the indulgence of readers of the 'coloured' style of his narrative in the interest of the 'amusement' of it for readers:

> If some parts of our narration may seem a little coloured, it is hoped that readers will be ready to extend the pardon which it is the custom to give to the writer who endeavours to interest the people whom he addresses ...
>
> The onerous and responsible task, which falls to the writer of such a book as ours, cannot be conceived from the mere reading of the plain and simple narrative, which is sent forth with the confident hope that it will repay readers who read for information, as well as those who read but for amusement.

As a reliable source of 'information', much less truth, about the *Mary Celeste* mystery, the bloated pages of Keating's book are a 'Macavity' of illusion. As for 'amusement', Keating's thunderously windbaggy writing attenuates even that modest prospect.

In its time, though, some reviewers considered the book a serious exposé of what Keating called the 'hoax' about the *Mary Celeste*, which solved her mystery. A *Yorkshire Post and Leeds Intelligencer* review of the book, on 15 May 1929, found that it was 'by no means an improbable story – indeed it is more probable than any other of the various explanations put forward during the past 50 years'.

Keating was, of course, the charlatan trump card in his own hoax: a perverted promise of truth he sustained by the quackery of 'alternative facts'.

Charles Edey Fay was having none of it, or him. In one of his *Sea Breezes* articles, in August 1950, he lamented the scurrilous scribblings of Keating in particular, who tainted the reputation of the honourable crew of the *Mary Celeste* by his characterisation of them as 'a mythical crew of quarrelling drunkards and bullies'.

Fay was insistent on restoring the dignity and humanity of those men who could no longer defend themselves from such inhumane and, worse, untruthful calumniation, not only for their sake but on behalf of their families and friends, left behind to read such mischievous malevolence. He lauded other writers, such as Lockhart and George Bryan, for their forensic discrediting of Keating's distorted and fabricated narrative.

But Fay, a decent and scrupulously truthful man, reserved his parting shot for Keating as an indecent and untruthful man for whom his disdain was absolute:

> The character of the Keating narrative may be briefly epitomized as follows:
> Here lies a book, of which it may be said
> It hoaxed the living and defamed the dead.

John Gilbert Lockhart, A Great Sea Mystery: The True Story of the Mary Celeste (1927)

Major, as he later became, J.G. (John Gilbert) Lockhart (1891–1960) was a man of considerable achievement. He was born in 1891, educated at Oxford, married in June 1937, and had two sons born during the Second World War, David in 1943 and Hugh in 1945, while serving as the First Secretary at the British Embassy in Washington, DC. In 1946 Lockhart was appointed an OBE (Officer, Order of the British Empire) and in 1952 a CBE (Commander, Order of the British Empire). He became a director at Philip Allan & Co., which published many of his sea books, and later a director at another publisher, Geoffrey Bles, which also published his works.

J.G. Lockhart was, by accounts, a sort of anti-Keating: a man of Christian faith, principles and moral probity. He wrote biographies of the theologian Charles Lindley Viscount Halifax, and Archbishop Cosmo Gordon Lang, as well as Cecil Rhodes, Sir Walter Scott and Napoleon Bonaparte. He seemed equally entranced by the sea and her mysteries and was the first author of a reliably sound account of the *Mary Celeste* mystery, *A Great Sea Mystery: The True Story of the Mary Celeste*, first published in 1927, with a series of follow-up titles into the 1950s.

Lockhart included the *Mary Celeste* mystery in an earlier book, *Mysteries of the Sea: A Book of Strange Tales*, in 1924. As a callow and susceptible novice to his subject then, he proposed that what happened on the *Mary Celeste* might be similar to what had happened on the brig *Mary Russell*, in 1828, 'whose Captain went off his head and, with the assistance of two apprentices, first bound and then butchered the greater part of his crew, two men, both badly injured managing to escape from him and to hide in the hold'.

Lockhart wrote in 1924 that 'the clue to my explanation is to be found in one small circumstance which has generally escaped notice'. That 'clue' was the harmonium in the cabin 'and several books, mostly of a religious character', which suggested there was on board the *Mary Celeste* someone who had become overwhelmed by a kind of 'religious mania'. And:

> Probably, the Captain was the man.

Capt. Briggs, Lockhart posited, 'was suddenly attacked by a terrible fit of homicidal religious mania. He became obsessed with the idea that it was his duty to release from the miseries of life his wife, his child, and the seven men of his crew.' Which he did. And then he proceeded to do himself in once he realised the nature of 'the gruesome task' he had undertaken. Why he might have 'for no apparent reason, thrown away the ship's chronometer and some of her papers' was a mystery: 'Who can fathom the motives of a madman?'

Hedging his bets at the end, Lockhart admitted: 'The theory, of course, is open to much fair criticism. But again, we can only guess.' And, of course, the true legacy of the *Mary Celeste* mystique is the iteration of one guess after another.

In *A Great Sea Mystery* (1927), his first book dedicated entirely to the *Mary Celeste*, Lockhart proffered that his 1924 'solution' was:

> ... merely conjecture, of which little more could be said than that, although there was not a lot of positive evidence in its support, it roughly accounted for most of the facts as I have given them ... Since the appearance of *Mysteries of the Sea*, however, I have accumulated much fresh material, and have had access to sources of information of the existence of which I was ignorant at the time of writing.

Lockhart debunked a number of tall tales in *A Great Sea Mystery*, including the Abel Fosdyk fiction, Capt. Lucy's story of 'Triggs', and the Lee Kaye/Keating yarn about the old cook, John Pemberton. Of the first two he concluded:

> I hope I have said enough to persuade the reader that Triggs is about as genuine a witness as Abel Fosdyk. Whether the leg that was pulled

> was that of Captain Lucy or of the editor of the London newspaper is a matter on which I would rather not hazard an opinion.

The Pemberton story, which had appeared a year earlier, was, he wrote, 'in my opinion, the most plausible of all the "Solutions" to the mystery of the *Mary Celeste*'. Under his forensic scrutiny, however, 'the story dissolves under test, and we are obliged to condemn as fiction this latest and most ingenious "solution" to the mystery of the *Mary Celeste*'. Still, it was, in his estimation, 'quite the best of all the sham solutions'.

Once he had confessed his own *mea culpa* 'solution' of 1924, Lockhart, in *A Great Sea Mystery*, and 'by way of amends', gave what he believed to be 'the true story'. This was the version set out by Dr Oliver Cobb, with whom he seemed to have been in contact – or whose research he was at least aware of – and agreed with by Charles Edey Fay.

Lockhart was not immune to the viruses of myth and fantasy about the *Mary Celeste*. In his last book, *The Mary Celeste and Other Strange Tales of the Sea*, in the early 1950s, he reprised his earlier narratives but kept to some well-worn 'alternative facts'. These included: that there was a mysterious German tanker on the scene of the *Dei Gratia*'s discovery; that all the *Mary Celeste*'s sails were set 'on the port tack' except her headsails 'being set to starboard'; that Capt. Morehouse went in the second boatload of men reboarding the *Mary Celeste*; and that there might have been the remains of a half-eaten breakfast on the cabin table, 'the accuracy of which I cannot guarantee'.

Not everything Lockhart wrote about the *Mary Celeste* mystery was entirely accurate. The resources and factual information available at the time were scant. The proliferation of 'fake news', misinformation and anecdotal myths tainted the records. It was a creditable achievement, under the circumstances, that he persevered to separate so much wheat from the chaff about the mystery. His *Mary Celeste* books, even with their factual delinquencies, are, to this day, amongst the most readable on the subject.

John Gilbert Lockhart died in London on 7 January 1960.

Charles Edey Fay, Mary Celeste: The Odyssey of an Abandoned Ship (1942)

Charles Edey Fay's *Mary Celeste* book. (Dover Publications edition, 1988)

The apex of Charles Edey Fay's professional life seems to have been his rise to the position of Vice-President of the Atlantic Mutual Insurance Company in New York, which insured the *Mary Celeste*'s 'freight on charter' for her 1872 voyage to Genoa. His birthdate is recorded as 26 May 1875, at Stamford, Connecticut, just outside New York City, and he died on 28 May 1957, aged 82, at Palm Beach, Florida. Whatever else occupied Mr Fay's life was not sufficiently momentous to trouble registering in public news outlets.

Not momentous except that Charles Edey Fay wrote the first detailed and factually accurate accounts of the *Mary Celeste* mystery, including the ship's background, the 1872 voyage and her crew, the Gibraltar hearings, and the various fictions and myths about her and 'solutions' to her mysterious abandonment.

That is Fay's public legacy: as the chronicler *par excellence* of the *Mary Celeste* phenomenon and in his dedication to the facts and clarity of the truth as far as anyone could know it at the time.

Fay's only book on the *Mary Celeste* was *Mary Celeste: The Odyssey of an Abandoned Ship* which he wrote as a commemoration of the Atlantic Mutual Insurance Company's centennial anniversary, in 1942. It was published as a special edition limited to 1,000 copies by the Peabody Museum, now the Peabody Essex Museum, of Salem, Massachusetts.

Dover Books, in New York, published an 'unabridged, slightly altered republication' of the original in 1988. Fay later, in 1950, wrote two articles about the *Mary Celeste* incident, in the August and September issues of the British magazine *Sea Breezes* dedicated to maritime and seafaring matters, which, frankly, are quite scarce for interested readers to access.

What singled out Fay's original *Mary Celeste* book in 1942 was its record of the factual evidence about his subject, drawing on all the sources he had available at the time. This included, for the first time, the Gibraltar Inquiry records – apparently an incomplete typewritten transcript Fay had obtained - and his personal research. Fay was appalled at all the cock-and-bull stories about the *Mary Celeste.* He reserved particular opprobrium for those writers, most notably Keating, who defamed and calumnied the members of the *Mary Celeste*'s crew, all of whom he characterised as honourable and seaworthy stalwarts.

The mass market Dover edition was a quite remarkable republication that included, amongst Fay's own narrative: copies and transcripts of numerous historical records; chronologies of events; an extensive Appendix of evidence, including 'Appendix C: Common Errors and Misconceptions'; and, most helpfully, a critical annotated chronology of published writings on the subject up to 1940. As an encyclopaedic compilation, it read nearly as dry as an insurance executive's audit report. As an audit of *Mary Celeste* facts, figures, and 'fake news', it was unparalleled amongst its peers. The original 1942 book was more readable. His later *Sea Breezes* articles of 1950 ploughed corners of the *Mary Celeste* mythoscape of fraud and flummery he had up till then disregarded.

Taken as a whole, Charles Edey Fay's canon of research and writings was in its time and remains even to this day a beacon of factual clarity: a benchmark source of reference to which later *Mary Celeste* writers owe a debt of gratitude.

George S. Bryan, Mystery Ship: The Mary Celeste in Fancy and in Fact (1942)

George S. (Sands) Bryan (1879–1943) was a heavyweight historical writer, especially on American subjects. He wrote about the assassination of Abraham Lincoln in *The Great American Myth* (1940), as well as biographies of Thomas Edison (1926) and the Texan revolutionary and US Senator Sam Houston (1917). He also wrote on less weighty matters in *The Camper's Own Book: A Handy Volume for Devotees of Tent and Trail* (1912), and *Too Much Salt*, 'a culinary comedy in one act' (1917). To cement his credentials as a factualist, he 'served on the staffs of the *New International Encyclopaedia* and the *Encyclopaedia Americana* and was managing editor of the *New Standard Encyclopaedia*'.

Cover of George Bryan's *Mystery Ship: The Mary Celeste in Fancy and in Fact.* (Lippincott Company, 1942)

So here was a man of erudition and letters, devoted to Fact and Truth and the censure of those who were not. His 1942 book, *Mystery Ship: The Mary Celeste in Fancy and in Fact*, is ample testimony to that aspiration. His erudition intruded in the reproduction of Conan Doyle's 'J. Habakuk Jephson's Statement' in the book. Towards the end, as Septimus Goring stated his ambition, Bryan helpfully inserted the unstated classical reference:

> 'I wish to be king over these fellows – not a very high ambition, certainly, but you know what Caesar said about being first in a village in Gaul ["I would rather be first in this town than second in Rome" – *Plutarch*].'

Bryan later added an insight from Conan Doyle about his short story:

> In his 'Memories and Adventures' he reminisced: 'What gave me great pleasure and for the first time made me realize that I was ceasing to be a hack writer and was getting into good company was when James Payn accepted my short story 'Habakuk Jephson's Statement' for *Cornhill*. I had a reverence for this splendid magazine with its traditions from Thackeray and Stevenson [Robert Louis Stevenson] and the thought that I had won my way into it pleased me even more than the cheque for £30, which came duly to hand.'

Mystery Ship: The Mary Celeste in Fancy and in Fact is a great and gratifying barrel of a tome. It adds considerable peripheral flesh to the core narrative of the *Mary Celeste* mystery by, for example, the inclusion of other commentators' critiques, sources of the taller tales – Hornibrook's giant octopus, for example – other mystery derelicts, and much else besides. It rolls through the usual yarns and conjectures and tall tales, and the imagined solutions, all with a critical eye for doing exactly what the title suggests: separating Fancy from Fact. As important, it was highly regarded by other serious *Mary Celeste* writers such as Charles Edey Fay. That in itself should be more than adequate recommendation for its worth.

A book reviewer in the *New York Times* of 26 April 1942 concluded:

> Mr. Bryan has a good time, and gives a good time to his readers, in recounting the wild tales, from semi-fiction to would-be hoax, which have gathered around the *Mary Celeste*. But when he looks at serious conjectures he considers them seriously. And he comes definitely to two which must be taken with seriousness, he says, 'as affording the most valid theories yet presented.'

Full stop. But the two 'conjectures ... which must be taken with seriousness' were: Dr Oliver Cobb's, as described earlier and subscribed to by others (fear of an alcoholic explosion); and a version of the same theory, but that the boatload of the *Mary Celeste* company was not driven out into the Atlantic to perish but was wrecked on nearby rocks. And, as a fully fledged factualist historian, Bryan backed up the theories with supportive evidence from other sources.

His account is one of the most solid and readable renditions of the *Mary Celeste* phenomenon.

Rupert Furneaux, *What Happened on the Mary Celeste* (1964)

This densely packed book covers a broad landscape of actual facts, 'fake news', 'alternative facts' and 'solutions' centred mainly on Dr Cobb's and Charles Edey Fay's versions and explanations about the *Mary Celeste* mystery. Rupert Furneaux (1908–81) was a prolific author of books on 'mysteries, murder trials and true crime'. His *What Happened on the Mary Celeste*, together with a piece he wrote for the *Illustrated London News*, of 2 November 1979, '*Mary Celeste*: The Truth', are of that forensic ilk.

At the end, however, Furneaux, having de-mythicised the mystery, reserves a few words to touch upon the humanity of the boatload of castaways' fears for their ship's destruction:

> So we destroy our gods. But, in mourning their passing, let us spare a thought for the poor people of the *Mary Celeste* at the awful moment of realisation, when they saw their staunch ship draw away leaving them tossing on the open sea. When they knew they were alone, their fears unfounded.

Gershom Bradford, The Secret of Mary Celeste and Other Sea Fare (1966)

In the July 1950 edition of the *American Neptune*, the quarterly journal of the then Peabody Museum, of Salem, Massachusetts, an article by Gershom Bradford III (1879–1978) was published titled '*Mary Celeste*: No, Not Again!' In it, Bradford posited the possibility, even likelihood, that a waterspout had struck the *Mary Celeste* as she was passing to the north-east of Santa Maria in the Azores. The accumulation of water in the ship caused the abandonment of her ten souls into the small boat. The 'confused sea' of the time could have overwhelmed the boat. And so Bradford mused finally that 'ten souls with their affections, hopes and sorrows were drawn back to the Parent-Spirit from a distressing tragedy of a swamped boat'.

Bradford's rather charming little tome (less than 100 pages), *The Secret of Mary Celeste and Other Sea Fare*, sixteen years later, reprised that theory. In it, Bradford reviewed and reconstructed the known *Mary*

Devastation of a ship at sea struck by a waterspout. (*Illustrated London News*, 22 April 1854)

Celeste facts. He used the evidence of the Gibraltar hearings to assess and dismiss previous theories about the cause of the abandonment, including the possibility of explosive alcoholic gases and the broken halyard notion suggested by Dr Cobb and Charles Edey Fay.

Bradford concluded, like others, that it was 'obvious that the crew abandoned her under some delusion of impending disaster'. Unlike others he reconstructed a scenario of a waterspout that 'engulfed [the vessel] in a screaming blast of wind and deluge of swirling water'. That 'deluge' accounted for the water within the *Mary Celeste* when the *Dei Gratia* found her. The ship's company would have soon perished, 'left castaways in a small boat on a rough sea', as the deserted *Mary Celeste* pulled away from them. Bradford finally explained how the ship could be found heading westwards on starboard tack by the *Dei Gratia*.

Gershom Bradford was from an old New England Yankee family, from Duxbury, between Boston and Cape Cod, with plenty of salt water mariners in his ancestral wake. He first went to sea aged around 19, in 1898, on 'a square-rigged schoolship' to train to be an officer on merchant ships, but spent most of his professional life as a scientist with the US Navy Hydrographic Office. Besides his *Mary Celeste* book, he authored: *The Whys and Wherefores of Navigation* (1918); *The Mariner's Dictionary* (1952); *A Glossary of Sea Terms* (1954); and *Yonder Is the Sea* (1959).

So Bradford knew his stuff about the wily ways and wherefores of the sea and seafarers. His waterspout theory in other hands might be discredited. But it was well caulked with the author's seafaring background and knowledge: what would be the most likely circumstances, and consequences, he asks, for the *Mary Celeste*'s experienced captain to abandon his ship? What would *he*, Gershom Bradford III, have done, he might as well have been asking.

Bradford died aged 98 on 12 April 1978.

Macdonald Hastings, Mary Celeste: A Centenary Record (1972)

The polymath English journalist, war correspondent, novelist, editor (of *The Strand* magazine from 1945 to 1950) and broadcaster Douglas Edward Macdonald ('Mac') Hastings (1909–82), father of the journalist Sir Max Hastings, wrote unarguably the most engaging of all *Mary Celeste* books, to mark the centenary of the 1872 mystery voyage.

Macdonald Hastings' *Mary Celeste: A Centenary Record.* (Michael Joseph, 1972)

His book reaches realms of originality that other *Mary Celeste* books do not, in at least two respects (three, if you count the cover picture, an original watercolour by John Worsley and one of the most accurate of all cover representations of the *Mary Celeste* when found by the *Dei Gratia*). The first is that he included personal correspondence from people that the journalist in him solicited and received that gave a personalised re-dimensioning of and insight into some of the nooks and crannies of the story. Secondly, his imagined reconstructions of certain events at the Gibraltar hearings featuring Mr Solly-Flood, and the Abel Fosdyk, J. Habakuk Jephson, Captain Lucy and Keating's 'Hoax' stories.

Hastings was fascinated in particular by Keating. Early in his research, he wrote, he 'became increasingly intrigued with the theories which have emerged, and the plain lies, in the convolutions of human minds. None, in that connection, is more fascinating than Laurence

J. Keating who wrote *The Great Mary Celeste Hoax*.' Amongst his portfolio of correspondence he had a letter about Keating from 'the late T.E. Elwell (4: 10: 57 [the date of the letter: 4 October 1957])', which minced no words in its opening statement:

> I knew Laurence Keating well. He was, or is, – I have no knowledge of his death – a liar, a confirmed plagiarist, and quarrelsome withal.

Elwell wrote the *Mary Celeste* piece titled 'A Chronometer Clue: The *Marie Celeste* Mystery', published by *Chambers's* in June 1923. Keating met Elwell around that time. In his letter to Hastings, Elwell wrote: 'Keating had never heard of the mystery, and said the whole thing was a fairy tale.' Scorched by some kind of literary jealousy, Keating apparently went off in a huff and wrote the sequence of spoofs centred around the fictional cook John Pemberton, from 1926, and ending with his 'Hoax' book in 1929.

In a letter to *Sea Breezes* magazine published in September 1950, Elwell remarked: 'I possess a copy of what I am sure is the most untrustworthy book on the subject of the *Mary Celeste*. It is "The Great Mary Celeste Hoax", by Laurence J. Keating, published in 1929.' Elwell asserted in the letter that the 'germ' of Keating's book had been Elwell's *Chambers's* article about 'A Chronometer Clue', hence the plagiarism claim.

Hastings offered a tantalising glimpse into Keating's character by quoting extracts from a letter Keating wrote to 'F.J. Lambert, an acquaintance he was clearly anxious to impress':

> The English book, *Great Mary Celeste Hoax*, appeared in 1929. It was an artless book written for artless men who live in Sailors' Homes and Ships, who know what it's talking about ... I assure you that nobody anywhere except Laurence Keating, has ever had an opportunity to 'research' the *Mary Celeste*, because all the relevant documents are the sole property of Laurence Keating's principals.

And Keating's opinion of Charles Edey Fay?

> Mr. Charles Edey Fay (Yank!!). What a Yank. It's not me, I assure you. I have not read Charles Edey.

'Not read Charles Edey Fay': so apparently, for Keating, it was enough that he was a 'Yank!!' to write him off. Hastings added:

> There was much more to Laurence Keating's letters. They are not worth recording. A psychiatrist might be interested in the inventions, which the fellow seems to have believed out of his own imagination ... [Keating] was one of those strange men who believed what he wanted to believe. The Irishry in him may have guided him as it guided Mr Solly Flood. His claim, like Mr Flood's, can be dismissed with a certain contempt.

In the opening salvoes of his book, Hastings wrote:

> Truth, there is no ultimate truth, exists only in what you believe ... The story of *Mary Celeste* is a classic not of what maybe happened but of what people for so many reasons for so many years have chosen to suppose did happen.

Much later in his book, and with the perspective of a hundred years' hindsight, he nailed the – or at least *an* – essence of the *Mary Celeste* phenomenon:

> The story of *Mary Celeste* is the more important because it is an example of what people will believe; and what others, for their own gain, will kid themselves into believing. *Mary Celeste* is a test of truth.
>
> Yet, examining the case, I am inclined to think that most people don't want truth. It is far more exciting, in a dull existence, to adventure into the realms of romance.

Brian Hicks, Ghost Ship: The Mysterious True Story of the Mary Celeste and Her Missing Crew (2004)

This book has the flair, floridity and fluency of style that one might expect of an experienced journalist. This is indeed the case: originally from Tennessee, Brian Hicks has been a journalist on the *Post and Courier* newspaper in Charleston, South Carolina, since 1997. His books include: *Raising the Hunley* (2002), co-written with Schuyler Kropf, about the history and salvage of a Confederate-era submarine; and *Into the Wind: Around Alone* (1999), with Tony Bartelme, about the 1998–99 Around Alone single-handed round-the-world yacht race that started life in 1982 as the BOC Challenge and had become the Velux 5 Oceans Race when it was last run in 2010–11.

Hicks reconstructs the *Mary Celeste* mystery with a journalistic enthusiasm for narrating a good human interest story. And he gets the facts right: about the history of the ship, including her post-1872 life, and of the families and individuals connected with her; the tall tales and 'alternative versions of the *Mary Celeste* legend', with, in some cases, historical context; and, in a chapter titled 'Into the Mystic', other sea mysteries.

His conclusion about the abandonment of the ship essentially agrees with Dr Cobb and Charles Edey Fay: that after the boatload of ten souls deserted the *Mary Celeste* for fear of an explosion by alcoholic vapours, attached by towline to the ship, 'the halyard broke', and 'they watched, helplessly, as the Ghost Ship sailed away without a soul on board'.

In the introductory paragraphs of his 'Notes', as an appendix, Hicks commented about the narrative style and journalistic-authorial integrity of his book:

> The quotes included in the narrative come from letters or court testimony; I did not put words into anyone's mouth. Their thoughts also came from letters, except in those instances when it was so obvious what they would have been thinking that I could safely infer.

I have added nothing to the *Mary Celeste*'s story. There has been enough of that already.

Paul Begg, Mary Celeste: The Greatest Mystery of the Sea (2005)

Reading Begg's book is like following a sniffer dog around the terrain of an air crash as it snuffles amongst the litter of evidence, burrows into the undergrowth of clues, and chases down leads into the backgrounds of victims and aircraft parts, rubber-necking bystanders and their speculative whisperings about the causes. The result is a book that throws light on the many alleyways, byways and cul-de-sacs of the *Mary Celeste* mystery, while laying out, examining, dissecting and digesting its central facts.

Paul Begg is acknowledged as a world authority on Jack the Ripper. He treats the *Mary Celeste* incident like the Ripper mystery: as a forensic accumulation of evidence and speculation, including notably the background of the ship and people associated with her, perusal of the 'wild and fanciful tales' about the mystery, derivative theatrical plays and media broadcasts, and 'other maritime mysteries' of abandoned phantom ships. He includes in the appendix, unapologetically, 'J. Habakuk Jephson's Statement' in its entirety, as 'probably the most influential tale ever written about *Mary Celeste*'.

The greatest single *factual* component of the book, in volume and value, is Begg's inclusion of a full verbatim transcript of the Gibraltar Inquiry, grammatical warts and all, including the personal testimonies amongst its formal statements and declarations. That, and the peripheral correspondence of the hearings' interlocutors – Solly-Flood, Consul Sprague and others – constitutes still the only bedrock of substance upon which insights into the mystery abandonment are grounded.

Although Begg takes no firm stand on one theory or another about the *Mary Celeste*'s abandonment, he hints at a preference in his final sentence, in view of the origin of the water found within the ship:

If it wasn't a waterspout, what could it have been?

Others

Elliott O'Donnell, *Strange Sea Mysteries*, Chapter 9: 'The *Marie Celeste*' (1926). Starting with O'Donnell's misnaming of the '*Marie Celeste*', 'the British barque *Dei Gratia*' and her 'Captain Boyce', followed by other fictitious 'facts', the author surmised that 'the most probable cause [of the *Mary Celeste* abandonment] was mutiny'.

Harold T. Wilkins, *Mysteries Solved and Unsolved*, Chapter 15: 'New Light on the *Mary Celeste*' (1959). Wilkins focused on critiquing the integrity of the Gibraltar Inquiry. Notes of personal correspondence, he wrote, disputed some critical parts of its evidence. His conclusion? 'My own theory that there is a criminological aspect of this mystery of the sea' is based on the 'trend of the evidence' from the Gibraltar Inquiry. The whole affair, he concluded, was 'Very strange!'

Len Ortzen, *Strange Mysteries of the Sea*, Chapter 3: 'The Ship That Sailed Herself' (1976). Most of Ortzen's compact reconstruction of the *Dei Gratia*'s encounter with the *Mary Celeste* and the Gibraltar Inquiry was factual. A slight early error is his assertion that 'the ship's master was Benjamin S. Briggs *of Marion, State of Maine* ...' The final words of his final paragraph – 'The most mysterious aspect of all, apart from what happened to the crew, is not so much that the *Mary Celeste* sailed seven hundred miles in less than ten days, apparently by herself, *but that it was on the course she was meant to be*' – likewise flaw an otherwise concise and quite good rendition of the *Mary Celeste* affair.

Stanley T. Spicer, *The Saga of the* Mary Celeste*: An Ill-fated Mystery Ship* (1993). This author is a serious historian of the *Mary Celeste*'s background, mystery and mythosphere, all in a compact fifty-page booklet of easy access for a quick and factual summary of the subject.

A.A. Hoehling, *Lost At Sea*, Chapter 1: '*Mary Celeste*: The Missing Log' (1984). Adolph August Hoehling (1914–2004) was a journalist who authored many books on military and maritime subjects. The *Mary Celeste* chapter in *Lost At Sea* is an intelligent and multi-questioning critique of the facts of the *Mary Celeste* mystery. One of the questions is the fate of the missing ship's log of the *Mary Celeste* from the very early days: 'Was it stolen? Was it destroyed?' The chapter is a quixotic quest for answers amongst the cracks and crevices of the mystery.

James Franklin Briggs, *In the Wake of the Mary Celeste* (1944). Capt. Benjamin Briggs' nephew, James Franklin Briggs (1878–1952), spent many years researching the *Mary Celeste* mystery, collecting a mass of information from personal and published sources. This thirty-five-page monograph, published as No. 74 in the series 'Old Dartmouth Historical Sketches', concludes:

> So ends the strange story of an unlucky ship. The little vessel's log is closed – but not the reader's interest.
>
> Still sails the *Mary Celeste* through waves of conjecture and waves of literature, and in her troubled wake still follow, unanswered, the questions of a great sea mystery.

Conclusion

Artful double-dealing to bowdlerise, manipulate, mangle and discredit the unimpeachable truth of facts was as prevalent in the creation of the *Mary Celeste* mythosphere as it is today. The twin faces of Fact and Truth have always been vulnerable to ignorance and fear, disfiguring them into 'alternative facts' and outright lies: myths – tall tales – deceptions.

For 150 years the *Mary Celeste* mystery has been dominated by a narrative of myths fed by an enduring mystique in pursuit of the truth – or, as often, a spin of the truth. Some mysteries, though, have no resolution: they prompt responses – 'solutions' – of degrees of probability or probity or nonsense, but reveal no answers. They stimulate a human craving for or belief in some kind of resolution, some closure, in the face of the sphinxian stare of the Great Unknown. Like some truths, they are simply unfathomable.

Mary Celeste is one of those.

The writer of a column in the *Nautical Gazette* of 1 May 1920, titled 'Another Unfathomed Ocean Mystery', about 'the recent appearance off the Scilly Isles of the three-masted schooner *Marion G. Douglas*, with her hull and rigging entirely undamaged and her cargo intact, but with not a living soul on board', acknowledged the ultimate inscrutability of the truth of the mystery:

> As to what happened to the crew of the *Marie Celeste*, one guess is just as good as another, for the truth is now probably in the sole keeping of the Recording Angel.

Notes

ORIGINS OF THE *MARY CELESTE*

1 Charles Edey Fay, *The Story of the Mary Celeste*.

THE 1872 MYSTERY VOYAGE

2 Charles Edey Fay, *Mary Celeste: The Odyssey of an Abandoned Ship*.

GIBRALTAR COURT OF INQUIRY

3 Charles Edey Fay, 'The Greatest Sea Mystery, Part 1', *Sea Breezes*, August 1950.
4 Charles Edey Fay, 'The Greatest Sea Mystery, Part 1', *Sea Breezes*, August 1950.
5 'Fearful Sufferings At Sea', *Manchester Evening News*, 15 March 1873.

YARNS, TALL TALES AND 'FAKE NEWS'

6 *Boston Post*, 24 February 1873.
7 *The Sun* [New York], 8 March 1873.
8 *New York Herald*, 15 March 1873.
9 *New York Herald*, 25 March 1873.
10 *The Sun* [New York], 12 March 1873.
11 *New York Herald*, 14 March 1873.
12 *Toronto Daily Mail*, 30 May 1883.

'J. HABAKUK STEPHSON'S STATEMENT', ANONYMOUS (ARTHUR CONAN DOYLE)

13 *Pall Mall Gazette* [London], 14 February 1884.
14 *Memphis Daily Appeal* [Memphis, Tenn.], 6 December 1885.

JACOB HAMMELL'S STORY

15 *Gloucester Citizen*, 17 May 1937.

'MYSTERY OF THE *MARY CELESTE*' BY JOHN BALL OSBORNE

16 *New York Tribune*, 1 February 1913.

FROM 'MARY SELLARS' TO 'MARIE CELESTE' TO MARY CELESTE

17 'A Sea Story Beloved of the Gullible Is Subjected to Cruel Analysis', *The Argus* [Melbourne], 2 October 1943.

18 *Nautical Gazette*, 1 March 1873.

DR OLIVER COBB AND CHARLES EDEY FAY

19 Dr Oliver W. Cobb, 'The "Mystery" of the *Mary Celeste*', *Yachting*, February 1940.

Bibliography

Every effort has been made to ascertain the copyright of all sources in the publication, and in the event of any omission the author requests to be contacted care of the publisher.

Books

Ansted, A., *A Dictionary of Sea Terms* (Glasgow: Brown, Son & Ferguson, 1920).

Begg, Paul, *Mary Celeste: The Greatest Mystery of the Sea* (Harlow: Pearson Education, 2005).

Bradford, Gershom, *The Secret of Mary Celeste and Other Sea Fare* (London: W. Foulsham, 1966).

Bryan, George S., *Mystery Ship: The Mary Celeste in Fancy and in Fact* (Philadelphia and New York: J.B. Lippincott, 1942).

Fay, Charles Edey, *Mary Celeste: The Odyssey of an Abandoned Ship* (Salem, Mass.: Peabody Museum, 1942).

Fay, Charles Edey, *The Story of the Mary Celeste* (New York: Dover Publications, 1988).

Furneaux, Rupert, *What Happened on the Mary Celeste* (London: Max Parrish, 1964).

Hastings, Macdonald, *Mary Celeste* (London: Michael Joseph, 1972).

Hicks, Brian, *Ghost Ship: The Mysterious True Story of the Mary Celeste and Her Missing Crew* (New York: Ballantine Books, 2004).

Hoehling, A.A., '*Mary Celeste*: The Missing Log', in *Lost at Sea: The Truth Behind Eight of History's Most Mysterious Ship Disasters* (Nashville, Tenn.: Rutledge Hill Press, 1984).

Keating, Laurence J., *The Great Mary Celeste Hoax* (London: Heath Cranton, 1929).
Lockhart, J.G., *A Great Sea Mystery: The True Story of the Mary Celeste* (London: Philip Allan, 1927; 1930 [Nautilus Library edition]).
Lockhart, J.G., *The Mary Celeste and Other Strange Tales of the Sea* (London: Rupert Hart-Davis, 1952).
Lockhart, J.G., 'The Mystery of the *Mary Celeste*', in *Mysteries of the Sea* (London: Philip Allan, 1924).
Lockhart, J.G., *True Tales of the Sea* (London: Quality Press, 1939).
O'Donnell, Elliot, 'The *Marie Celeste*', in *Strange Sea Mysteries* (London: John Lane The Bodley Head, 1926).
Ortzen, Len, 'The Ship that Sailed Herself', in *Strange Mysteries of the Sea* (New York: St Martin's Press, 1976).
Spicer, Stanley T., *The Saga of the Mary Celeste: Ill-fated Mystery Ship* (Halifax, Nova Scotia: Nimbus, 1993).
Wilkins, Harold T., 'New Light on the *Mary Celeste*', in *Mysteries: Solved and Unsolved* (London: Odhams Press, 1958).

Magazine and Journal Articles (in chronological order)

Anonymous [Arthur Conan Doyle], 'J. Habakuk Jephson's Statement', *Cornhill Magazine*, January 1884.
Hornibrook, J.L., 'The Case of the *Marie Celeste*: An Ocean Mystery', *Chambers's Journal*, 17 September 1904.
McGrath, P.T., 'Terror of the Sea', *McClure's Magazine*, May 1905.
'The Greatest Mystery of the Sea: Can You Solve It?', *The Strand*, July 1913.
'The Mystery of the *Marie Celeste*', *Nautical Magazine*, October 1913.
'The *Marie Celeste*: The True Solution of the Mystery?' (Abel Fosdyk's story), *The Strand*, November 1913.
'The *Marie Celeste*: A Solution' (Capt. Lukhmanoff's story), *Nautical Magazine*, December 1913.

'The *Mary Celeste*', *Nautical Gazette*, 17 December 1913.
'The *Mary Celeste* Mystery Explained', *Nautical Gazette*, 24 December 1913.
'Sequel to the *Mary Celeste* Mystery', *Nautical Gazette*, 31 December 1913.
'Mystery Ships' (including *Mary Celeste*), *Chambers's Journal*, 22 October 1921.
Elwell, T.E., 'A Chronometer Clue: The *Marie Celeste* Mystery', *Chambers's Journal*, 9 June 1923.
Kaye, Lee (alias Laurence J. Keating), 'The Truth About *Marie Celeste*: A Survivor Story' (John Pemberton's story), *Chambers's Journal*, 26 July 1926.
Hornibrook, J.L., 'New Light on the *Marie Celeste* Case', *Chambers's Journal*, March 1933.
Gould, Lieut.-Com. R.T., 'Mystery of the *Mary Celeste*', *Shipping Wonders of the World*, 19 January 1937.
Cobb, Dr. Oliver W., 'The "Mystery" of the *Mary Celeste*', *Yachting*, February 1940.
Briggs, James Franklin, 'In the Wake of the *Mary Celeste*', Old Dartmouth Historical Sketches, No. 74, 1944.
Orsborne, Dod, 'The Phantom Islands', edited by Joe McCarthy, *Life*, 6 December 1948.
Fay, Charles Edey, 'The Greatest Sea Mystery', *Sea Breezes*, August (Part 1) and September (Part 2) 1950.
Furneaux, Rupert, '*Mary Celeste*: The Truth', *Illustrated London News*, Christmas number, 2 November 1979.

Thrilling Tales of the Sea

978-0-7509-9084-4

978-0-7509-9085-1

978-0-7509-9086-8

978-0-7509-9087-5